Shieldmaiden

The Devin Snyder Story

by Dan Folts

For Kate Ott,

In honor of

Devin's service.

DFolts

Feb. 2019

For my family.

Dramatis Personae

Devin A. Snyder,	*a modern shieldmaiden* *
Dineen Snyder,	*her mother*
Ed Snyder,	*her father, a sailor*
Derek	
Natasha	*her siblings*
Damien	
Danette McInnis,	*her aunt, Dineen's sister*
Greg McInnis,	*her uncle*
Judge Ron Snyder,	*her great-uncle, Ed's uncle*
Julie Martin,	*her soccer coach*
Jeff Englert,	*her track coach*
Tom Cox,	*the former village mayor*
Jack Zigenfus,	*the former town supervisor*
Emily May	
Tyler Austin	
Dave Saxton	*high school classmates, teammates, and friends*
Alyssa Englert	
Mikayla Sick	
Meaghan Oas	
Jessica Jeffords,	
Scott Enlow	
Stacey Jordan	*Army buddies and friends*
Jeremy Johnson	
Josh Pruitt	

* a woman warrior, from the Old Norse *skjaldmaer*

5

Author's Introduction

This is *one* story of *one* soldier.

And like a story, our lives unfold without knowing how they will end. War, such a powerful part of human life that it was deified twice by ancient Western cultures, adds another violent, chaotic layer to the unknown. Often called a theater when referring to different battle zones, there may not be a more accurate metaphor for war. It may not play out in exactly five acts, but it is most certainly a tragic production. Like a Greek tragedy, the story of Devin Snyder has always seemed to me a convergence of unstoppable forces and at it's center, a tragic heroine.

Some of those forces might include the Cold War, the Soviet Union's failure in Afghanistan in the 1980s, the rise of Islamic Fundamentalism throughout the Middle East, the attacks on 9/11, and the resulting War on Terror. At home, like Newton's 3rd Law in the political realm, we've seen the rise of nationalism from the ashes of Washington and Wall Street. Something deeply rooted came to express itself collectively. Those against the wars fought for peace. But the appeal to look at what is common among humanity was drowned out to a significant degree by a primal desire for revenge, lasting more than a decade.

The arc of justice might be long, but at its root is that very common human desire to defend the tranquility of the tribe and, if necessary, to even the score. It is an emotionally-invested sense of justice. This feeling is compounded in young people by the adolescent desire to prove oneself, to establish one's own identity, and to seek adventure. It was, and is, a type of hubris that is preyed upon by politicians who so eagerly send young men and women to war in order to gratify their own hubris. If there is a swamp in Washington, it is a swamp of pride. On the battlefield, it is a mire in which soldiers show loyalty, valor, and mercy, some of our best attributes. Such is the frustrating paradox of human existence, evil is found in good, and good in evil. It can be hard to tell where one ends and the other begins.

I suppose that is what makes drama so satisfying: clarity. As audience members, we are able to watch a character meet his end due to his own moral failings and see it clearly. The Greek tragedians instruct the audience about violations of the moral code and warn us that the Gods are quick to take offense. Unlike the dramas of our lives, we are able to judge a character's actions from afar and weigh the outcome. We see that justice is served, yet the Gods are unfair. A high price is always paid for victory, and in defeat the vanquished display such nobility that it is also tragic. Art falls short of imitating life in that sense because it does not imitate confusion. The audience can put themselves in the character's place without having to act, so the emotional investment only goes so far; thus the audience does not have the limitation of subjectivity and personal bias with which to contend.

Through tragedy we learn how not to behave, how not to rush to judgment, and how important it is to consider others. But we also learn that to a certain extent we are not in control of our lives. Many outside influences, including the actions of juvenile and petty gods, toss us around like ships on the wine-dark sea.

Despite the redeeming quality of her valor, Devin's death was painful, one that was mourned by everyone who knew her. We had to force ourselves to accept it, in one way or another. Politics didn't matter. Those who were in favor of the long war in Afghanistan thought it was a necessary evil and saw her as making a heroic sacrifice to help protect her country. Those who were against the war saw her death as a tragic waste of a young person's life. Everyone mourned, shedding tears in public or bearing it stoically.

After talking with her family and many close friends, it became clear the central characteristic that made Devin unique. Yes, she sought adventure, and that may be why she was a trailblazer in the trend toward women being allowed in combat zones. But her most important trait was her determination. Her mother, in attempting to let go of her child's life path, as all parents eventually must do, told me, "It's what she wanted to do."

That phrase sums up Devin's determination, but what is tragic is that her best characteristic, in the sense of a Greek tragedy, became her tragic flaw. There is no way that her story can be viewed as triumphant, but we can admire her for who she was, and for those characteristics that she embodied. That admiration can offer some solace.

Part 1: Innocence

"He has made everything beautiful in its time; also he has put eternity into man's mind, yet so that he cannot find out what God has done from the beginning to the end" –Ecclesiastes 3:11

Chapter 1: Homecoming

Roads run parallel to rivers the way memories run parallel to absence.

Ed Snyder had decided not to re-enlist in the Navy and he and his pregnant wife, Dineen, and their three children were riding from the airport in Rochester, NY to their hometown of Cohocton, NY. They followed the Genesee River, driving south on I-390.

As they passed the small villages, moving upward toward the end of the tributary near Dansville, Ed might have noticed the red buds breaking on the tops of red maple trees. He might have seen the gray, fuzzy buds of the quaking aspen, or the bright yellow of the weeping willow branches. There were undoubtedly birdsongs, the sound of rushing creeks, and the warmth of sunshine.

It was a ride that the Snyders barely remember. They were tired from traveling and the young children were lulled by the repetitive sound of the tires hitting small bumps on the surface of the interstate as they came up over the hill and down into the Cohocton River Valley.

They were coming home from Norfolk, VA, where Ed had been stationed in the Navy for nearly a decade. As a young man, Ed used the Navy as many young people do: as a way of getting out of their hometown and seeing the world. He visited many distant port countries and cities. In Rio de Janeiro, the ship anchored in full view of the famous Christ the Redeemer statue. They stopped in Colombia, as well as many ports in the Caribbean such as Saint Croix and Saint Thomas, and sailed the east coast of the US. In Europe, Ed stayed in Germany for about ten days. Being of German descent, he enjoyed a sort of genetic homecoming. The thought led him to imbibe in the many Germanic cultural offerings.

"I think Germany is the only place you can get a beer with your breakfast," said Ed. "I really liked Germany."

Ed and Dineen had been sweethearts since high school. They were together but not married and Dineen had their son, Derek, when she was 18. She went back and forth between Norfolk, VA and New York when she needed family support. Being a mom, she found, was sometimes a lonely occupation.

International phone calls were, at the time, too expensive for frequent or lengthy conversations. Once, Ed called from Italy. They seemed to talk for only five minutes or so, but the phone bill the next month was astronomical.

"We'd only plan that like once throughout his deployment because obviously you can't afford that every week," said Dineen.

They wrote letters frequently and the time passed.

"You didn't pick up the phone and call every chance you got," said Dineen. "Being social with people just wasn't what it is today. So yeah, it was hard, but you kind of become more independent."

One day, March 13th, 1984, Dineen got a call from Ed.

"I'm coming home this weekend," he said. "We're getting married."

At that time you had to have a blood test to get a marriage license. So he had called early to be sure she could get one.

"So he came home on Friday," said Dineen. "We got married Saturday. He left Sunday and he deployed Monday for six months."

For about four or five years, it was mostly just Dineen and little Derek. They were a military family. They had an apartment in the city of Norfolk, but city life did not suit Dineen much.

"I'm a country girl," said Dineen. "I come from a rural area so at night in a city, you hear things, and it just makes you nervous."

Then, on December 1, 1987, while Ed was out to sea, Natasha was born. Ed found out the next day when the captain gave him a balloon, congratulating him on the birth of his daughter.

"Natasha and I always joke, even to this day," said Ed. "Because I got the notice on December second and she was born on December first, I always say her birthday is December second and she always says it's December first."

"She was probably about four months old when he got to see her for the first time," remembered Dineen.

"She was walkin' and talkin' in Virginia Beach when we lived there," Ed recalled.

After Natasha was born, military life continued.

"It was tough having the kids and him being gone," said Dineen. "It's a struggle. Just so many things you face on your own."

For six years, Ed was on the USS Iowa. A former WWII warship, the Iowa was part of the United States' Pacific fleet. It served in the Korean War and was then was maintained as a reserve ship. Later, in response to a buildup in the Soviet navy, the ship was moved to an active status. This is when Ed Snyder was on it. His travels took him to many other distant places.

He skied in the Netherlands and felt the hot sun on his face in Mexico. He even went to Antarctica.

"It was cold... But down in the fire room of the U.S.S. Iowa it's always a hundred degrees, hundred-ten degrees."

The ships massive 16-inch guns blew away icebergs as target practice.

It was those exact 16-inch guns that would later be a source of controversy for the USS Iowa.

It was April of 1989. They were off the Virginia capes at the time, and a high-ranking officer was observing their qualification rounds, when each gun is fired to show that they're on target. It's a test of safety, accuracy of the weapon, and competency of the crew.

"Of course, sixteen-inch guns are ancient, old, so your gunpowder is huge. It's probably been sitting around for years and year and years. I think that the problem was the gunpowder was damp, wet, whatever. When the ram rammed the gunpowder, that's when the spark exploded."

Somehow, and there are competing theories on this, the breach of turret two was open and the explosion rocked the ship, killing forty-seven.

Ed recalls the disaster:

"We were going twenty-two knots through the water. I remember it to this day. Twenty-two knots through the water. When the captain rings up an all stop, your recorder would go 'chingching'. You'd hear that and that's it. Everything comes to a stop. Down in the fire room you've got burners to kick in and kick out and you've got steam going up. You've got to stop that steam going to the main engine because if you don't you've got safeties lifting and you could lose fires in the boiler and just everything could happen. That day everything went right. We came to a complete stop. Captain come across the one MC saying that there was an explosion, turret two, center gun, general quarters, general quarters. And then everybody went to their general quarters station and then they came back on."

As the sailors got to their stations, the captain began giving out orders to save the ship.

"He took charge and got the firefighters to put water onto the turret and start shutting hatches. Even if somebody was behind that hatch in that room, you shut that hatch and flooded the room. There was live gunpowder in there. So he flooded the room even though somebody was behind the door wanting to get out or whatever. Your job is to shut that door and flood it. There's lots of guys that shut the doors knowing that there was another guy or two, three guys behind that door wanting to get out. If you open the door you're risking the whole ship."

Afterwards, Ed and the others had to recover the bodies of those they lost.

"After that they drained the bulk heads and we had to go in and get the guys that were in the turret and that's how they died, holding on to something or whatever... Pry the dead bodies off and put them into body bags, and of course the body bags would go into the locker right where we slept. It's a smell you'll never forget. Or a sight you'll never forget."

The crew stayed aboard the ship for two days as the naval officers tried to piece together what had happened. Then they came back into port and families were let on the ship.

"Usually, when they pulled back in, seeing the ship come in from any other deployment you could see the excitement," remembered Dineen. "Everybody waiting to get off and see their families. On his it was just gloom and doom."

"The turret was still the way it was when it blew up," remembered Ed. "Raised in the air for investigation purposes."

"They had it covered with a black drape too when they came back in," said Dineen, "because obviously you don't want the newscasters to see it or anything."

They came off the ship for a couple of days but then went right back out to sea. Ed didn't speak of the incident for a long time.

Back on the ship, the mood was different than before.

"I don't think anybody said anything to anybody," said Ed.

After some time, Ed and the others did experience some healing. It helped to have friends who were there. Bearing a tragic experience brings people closer together, he learned.

But 1989 had turned out to be an eventful year. About a year before their daughter Devin Snyder was born, the Soviet army left Afghanistan, beaten by the US-backed mujahedeen. Also in that year, the National Islamic Front (NIF) in Sudan, a partner of al-Qaeda, came to power by military coup. That November, pro-unification protesters climbed up the Berlin wall and pounded on it with sledgehammers in full view of news cameras. These seemingly disparate events would have profound consequences for the Snyders.

The previous year, Osama bin Laden founded al Qaeda or "The Base." It was made up of former mujahedeen, experienced in guerrilla warfare, insurgency, and terrorism and eager to continue the fight against influence from outside of the Middle East, especially the West. They were supported by Iran and Hezbollah, but not by the Saudi regime, who thought their radical activities could destabilize their own rule. The Saudis even revoked Bin Laden's passport to try to slow any international organizing.

When Ed returned from the USS Iowa tragedy unscathed, things returned to what we would call a normal family life. He and Dineen were then living in an off-base apartment in Virginia Beach while he had shore duty. Dineen, now pregnant with Devin, had her two oldest children, Derek and Natasha, at home. Ed would report to his duties and return in the evening. Having been so close to death made life much sweeter.

In 1990, five days before Devin was born, Iraq invaded Kuwait, initiating the Persian Gulf War. Like much of the Middle East, Kuwait was first part of the Ottoman Empire, then part of the British Empire after World War I. But it had always been part of what was considered "Iraq," though in the centuries of the Ottoman Empire, there was no nationalist identity. In fact, Kuwait did not become an independent state until 1961. Before that, the ruling family of Kuwait, the al-Sabah family, had been in power since 1899 under the protection of the British. Efforts by Iraqis to "reunite" Kuwait with Iraq failed in both the 1930s and the 1960s due to British military and diplomatic involvement and the al-Sabah family remains in power to this day.

That pattern of intervention and support for the al-Sabah dynasty continued as British power waned and American power waxed. When the Iranian Revolution took place in 1979, the US looked to the increasingly wealthy Iraq for an Arab partner and found it in Saddam Hussein. Hoping to capitalize on the internal turmoil of Iran, Iraq invaded in 1980, starting eight years of war. The war itself was categorized by great WWI-style brutality, including the use of trench warfare and chemical weapons. Both the United States and Kuwait helped fund Iraq's efforts in the war, and in that time, Kuwait, allegedly using slant-drilling technology from the US, began to tap the Rumaila oil field.

The al-Sabah family of Kuwait had become extremely wealthy selling some of that oil at below OPEC prices to the west[1] and had invested a good amount of that wealth, maybe as much as $40 billion, in the United States stock markets.[2] With that much money intertwined in the US financial sector and oil continuing to be exported from Kuwait, the first Bush administration felt that the US *had* to intervene when Saddam's forces invaded Kuwait on August 2, 1990.

Five days later, on August 7, 1990, Devin Snyder was born. That day, Ed remembers, they were at the hospital and the Yankees were playing the Seattle Mariners. Kevin Maas hit his twelfth homerun in the Yankees' 3-1 win. Ed was watching the game on the TV, thinking there was a good amount of time before the baby would come.

16

Suddenly, Dineen spoke up.

"Ed, I think I need to push," she said.

"No you don't," replied a confident Ed. "They just checked you. You're fine."

"No, Ed, I think I really need to push."

Ed went to get the nurse, and before the doctor could get there, Devin was born. She was six weeks early and weighed six pounds.

"I got to hold her before they put her in the machine," remembered Ed. "She thinks that's why we were so close."

"Yeah, I do," said Dineen. "She would even say it. 'Ed's my favorite'. I knew she was kidding but she would say it all the time."

Evidence suggests that newborn-parent bonding occurs best when the parent, usually the mother, has some sort of skin-to-skin contact with the baby, like nursing or just cuddling. But experts also say that fathers bond with children in a similar way, often through play, due to the release of oxytocin, a brain compound known as the "attachment chemical."[3] Science aside, Ed, after seeing so much loss, was on land this time and able to see his daughter born. He was given hope.

Her older brother, Derek, wanted to name her Ariel after The Little Mermaid, the blockbuster children's movie at the time. So they named her Devin Arielle.

Soon it was discovered that some of the fighting between Iraq and Kuwait had spilled over into Saudi territory. The next day, August 8, in an address to the nation, President George H.W. Bush emphasized our relationship with Saudi Arabia, saying:

"The sovereign independence of Saudi Arabia is of vital interest to the United States. This decision, which I shared with the congressional leadership, grows out of the longstanding friendship and security relationship between the United States and Saudi Arabia. U.S. forces will work together with those of Saudi Arabia and other nations to preserve the integrity of Saudi Arabia and to deter further Iraqi aggression. Through their presence, as well as through training and exercises, these multinational forces will enhance the overall capability of Saudi Armed Forces to defend the Kingdom."

He also added that he hoped that oil-producing countries would "do what they can to increase production in order to minimize any impact that oil flow reductions will have on the world economy."

It seemed that the concerns were not limited to Kuwait, but included the possibility of Iraq invading other countries in the region, perhaps to establish the pan-Arab state by force where others had failed with diplomacy. Other targets might include Israel. Thus began Operation Desert Shield, aimed at containing Iraqi aggression, the very aggression that we sought to encourage when it was focused on Iran.

Bin Laden saw this as a deep offense, that western-allied forces would be present in the land of the two most holy Islamic sites, Mecca and Medina. He wanted the mujahedeen, the "Afghan Arabs," who had been so successful in defeating the Soviets, to be the only army that defended against Hussein. But because the Iraqi army had grown so strong in the wake of the war with Iran, it would have been risky for Saudi Arabia to defend itself against Hussein and his nationalist Ba'ath Party. Bin Laden spoke out and was later exiled by the Saudi government. Apparently he valued the Western ideal of free speech, while at the same time declaring us to be the great evil. It was around this time that he moved to Sudan, where the National Islamic Front would shelter him.

It wasn't until January of 1991 that Operation Desert Storm began and by the time the war was over in March, about half a million coalition troops had flooded the region, including about forty thousand female US soldiers. When the war was over, Iraq had gained no new lands, but had the second strongest military in the Middle East, after Israel. It had a tremendous war debt and resentment toward Kuwait for what it considered "stealing" oil. Saddam's forces were defeated and President George H. W. Bush and his commanders made the decision to leave Hussein in power, stopping short of Baghdad. He did so, according to his 1998 memoir, *A World Transformed*, because he knew that "We would have been forced to occupy Bagdad and, in effect, rule Iraq... there was no viable 'exit strategy' we could see... Had we gone the invasion route, the United States could conceivably still be an occupying power in a bitterly hostile land."[4]

Chapter 2: The Cohocton River Valley

As Ed and Dineen returned to the Cohocton Valley, they remembered that it was no longer the same as the Cohocton of their childhoods.

The landscape was the same, largely, as it had been for millennia. The region surrounding the Cohocton Valley in the Southern Tier of New York State is greatly indebted to the last Ice Age. Its hills, valleys, and waterways were all formed from that continental turmoil. It is a place where mountain met glacier, like the scene of an ancient battle of giants. They left their mark. Some those marks, which have a sort of radial symmetry, faintly look like a handprint, and thus are called the Finger Lakes. Cohocton is part of the long river system just a few miles south of the Finger Lakes. It is part of the northernmost sub-region of Appalachia, in the far away rolling foothills of the great eastern mountain chain.[5]

Coming down the hill, from the interstate and into the village proper, church signs advertise roast pork and spaghetti dinner fundraisers. At the lowest elevation in the village is a green steel bridge spanning the Cohocton River.

Winding its way from the hills of Springwater, along Tabors Corners Road in Wayland, through the Hamlet of Atlanta, and finally through the very center of the Village of Cohocton, the Cohocton River is part of one of the great Eastern watersheds, leading southeast toward the Chemung River, between the hills of the Allegheny Plateau, then to the Susquehanna River and, eventually, to Chesapeake Bay. Historically, the creeks and rivers were the original World Wide Web.

To the settlers, the river was a way in. To others it is a way out.

Well before the first white settlers, the Cohocton River valley was part of a vast network of foot trails used by native tribes, mostly the Senecas, for travel, trade, hunting, and later for traveling east to meet with the representatives of the United States. Essentially, our best roads today are built on top of old Indian trails along the waterways. In or out, the Cohocton River and its tributaries are a crossroads.

This is particularly evident when one considers the original name for the area, "Conhocton." (The "n" was dropped from the native name due to bureaucratic misspelling). The name is Seneca for "the place of coming together." It is sometimes translated as "tree in the river," but it may be closer to a metaphor along the lines of "fork in the road." However, when taken too literally conjures up the image of a log sticking out of some muddy water. The name may in fact literally translate to "tree in the river," but may truly mean that Cohocton is the place where many waterways converge, and if seen from the hills above, at the bottom of the green valley there appears a shining form that looks much like branches of a tree coming together to form a "trunk," or the Cohocton River.

A New York State historic marker on the south end of the Village of Cohocton reminds visitors of the region's violent history. It reads "Historic Cohocton Valley. Seneca Indians inhabited this area until 1779 when their towns and cornfields were destroyed by the Sullivan-Clinton Expedition."

That campaign, led by General Sullivan and ordered by General Washington, was intended to destroy the Haudenosaunee (Iroquois).[6] Following the Susquehanna north from Pennsylvania, Sullivan and Clinton met forces at Tioga, numbering around 5,000 troops, then marched west into the heart of Six Nations territory. It resulted in the destruction of over forty villages and 160,000 bushels of corn, the staple of their winter diet.[7]

About 3,000 Haudenosaunee made the long trek to Fort Niagara, where they spent the winter as refugees. The sudden influx of people brought the fort's population to over 5,000.[8] After that desperate winter, during which many starved at Niagara, some natives moved back to the area and rebuilt a life of some kind, living with the settlers, becoming more like them. Others moved on. Some sought revenge and as soon as the next year, the raids continued. Violence was a part of frontier life for some time, but the Six Nations Confederacy had been broken by the war and shattered by the Sullivan-Clinton Campaign.

Most Haudenosaunee people had left the Cohocton Valley by 1815.

This tragic downfall of an indigenous people opened up Western New York for settlement. The first large section was given directly to veterans of the Revolution. A section called the Central New York Military Tract, east of Cohocton, was given to US soldiers in 100-acre plots. It constituted an area about the size of Rhode Island and Delaware combined.

Many of the resulting towns were inspired by the Greek Revival period. Buildings with fronts of Greek pillars sprouted up in logging towns, looking like the façades of the Temple of Zeus amongst the fields of corn. Many of the towns and cities were named for cities in classical antiquity, like Ithaca, Rome, Attica, Utica, Troy, Sparta, and Marathon. Others were named for poets, like Ovid, Homer, and Virgil, or warriors, like Hector.[9] All pointed toward the spirit of conquest and the glory of victory, as well as the high ideals of the ancient world, one that the new settlers hoped to resurrect. This naming trend, it might be argued, could be considered an early form of real estate marketing, but what the settlers found in the land that was newly cleared of its inhabitants, was a vast fertility that gave them hope for the future.

In *The Power of Myth*, journalist Bill Moyers interviews Joseph Campbell, expert in myth and religion, about how landscapes affect people. He claims that new settlers create "sacred sites" by "investing the land with spiritual powers." He called the practice "land-claiming" in which settlers turn the land into "a place of spiritual relevance."

"Our pilgrim fathers, for example," continued Campbell, "named sites after Biblical Centers. And somebody in upper New York State had *The Odyssey* and *The Iliad* in his mind—Ithaca, Utica, and one classical name after another."[10]

The land was then settled and, since it was connected to the Susquehanna watershed, became an important trade route for the pre-Erie Canal frontier.

Logging was the first profitable enterprise in Cohocton. The hillsides bore old growth white pine in abundant groves. Natives using controlled fires cultivated these and other useful trees in the forests. Known as "The Great Tree of Peace" to the Haudenosaunee, they became abundant timber for the new settlers,

21

who were able to float the logs down river, as far east as necessary in order to sell them. The forests were soon clear-cut, and the former wildlife habitat became a pretty strictly human, agricultural habitat.[11] The Town of Cohocton was formed from that in 1805.

One of the prominent names in Cohocton of that time is the Laroux family. They built a large colonial-style house in the center of town and became a sort of self-made upper class of the valley. Mr. Laroux, one of the founding members of the United States Republican Party, brought in the first steam pump to irrigate crops from the river. Many German and Swedish immigrants began moving to the area to farm. The railroad came. They became known for buckwheat. Laroux buckwheat mill was opened in 1866 and the sacks of buckwheat flower went to general stores and kitchen shelves across the region.

Because the area was a major travel corridor, there were many stagecoach stops for people heading west. These places served as rest stops, of sorts, for the road-weary traveller or the worn out horse.

A sawmill was built, and the logging continued. More settlers moved into or moved through the area. There was an influx of people, so Cohocton became a rural, but busy and bustling place. The soil was deep and fertile in the valley and the farms there became known for their potatoes.

Potatoes are still a major crop in the area. Some farmers sell their potatoes to chip companies and others sell bags of new red potatoes and salt potatoes at roadside stands.

Sawmills were still a profitable business when Dineen was growing up. In fact, she grew up in a sawmill family. Her grandfather, Reuben Kanaval, owned a mill with his older brother, Ed, and made a life in the Cohocton Valley for himself and his family. They milled timber into building material for local homes and outbuildings until 1993. It was a family business that started with Ed and Reub Kanaval working in other lumber mills as young men, gaining experience and expertise. Days started early, and they worked year round, ten hours a day, six days a week. In 1940, they ventured out on their own and started Kanaval Brothers Lumber Company. After moving to several locations and a despite a devastating fire, they rebuilt and ran the company successfully for five decades, employing themselves and, later, their sons as well, including Reuben Kanaval's son Anthony, Devin's maternal grandfather, for a short time.

To make a life from the unforgiving land is both dangerous and painful. Many things can go wrong. The hills, so picturesque from the Cohocton Valley floor, create both obstacles and advantages for the logger. He must climb up old, mucky logging roads with horses, hitches, and saws to the big timber, gauge the slope of the hill and the lean of the tree and make his best guess about where it will fall. Two of them have to pull the crosscut saw back and forth until a wedge is removed from the direction of the fall. Then the back cut, the cracking of the last fibers in the cold quiet wood, and the final *whoosh* of the treetop as it falls.

From there the hills give the logger an advantage: gravity. After de-branching the tree, the resulting log can be skidded downhill to a roadside much more easily. But that is no solace. The job must continue, and the log pile must grow greater every day for the job to pay off.

How many times did Dineen and Danette, Devin's mother and aunt, see their grandfather tired from work? They doubtfully saw him otherwise. His hands, calloused and creviced, were the outward indicator of his toil. The ache in his elbows, shoulders, and back were invisible to the young girls.

"My grandfather had nothing coming here," remembers Danette. "If you know anything about sawmill people, they're kind of rough and don't have a lot and they work paycheck to paycheck. He and uncle Ed just worked really hard and I think they were looked up to in the community."

"[Reuben] lived a tough life. He grew up tough," said Greg, Danette's husband, who once worked at the mill. "They'd be in the woods all day in the winter and the bean sandwiches, which was all they had to eat, would be frozen."

"He loved his kids," said Danette. "He had two boys and he had a daughter. His daughter ended up being mentally handicapped. They kept her at home until she was about seven. She almost got hurt when she wandered into the mill one day so they decided they needed to do something different. They put her in a home, which they thought was the best place for her to keep her safe. I think that always kind of hurt him because he didn't have his little girl."

When Dineen and Danette's parents first got married, they lived in a small trailer in front of the mill. Then Anthony Kanaval bought property on a nearby country road, built a house using rough sawn lumber from the mill, and moved in with his wife and two girls there. But moving a few miles away did not mean the family grew apart.

"My grandma and grandpa would come up once a week and they'd bring a half gallon of ice cream and bring us all Snickers bars and just hang out with us for a few hours in the evening, so we were all very close with them," said Danette. "Because they didn't have much, every year Grandma and Grandpa would take some of the grandchildren to get new winter coats and the next year they'd take the other ones to get new winter coats. It was kind of a family tradition they did."

"Reub was kind of a rough redneck, tough, salt of the earth guy, but a gentleman, and a smart investor too," said Greg. "Two opposites that came together in one man."

"They were good people," said Danette. "Grandma didn't have a lot growing up either. She came from potato farmers I believe and her parents were a lot older. She and grandpa got married and made their way. She was a lady. She never talked badly about anybody. She was respectful. I spent a lot of time down there because I'd go down on Saturdays and she would pay me to clean for the day so I could earn a little spending money."

"I worked there probably until I was eighteen or nineteen," said Danette. "I was very fortunate in that respect because I got to know her a lot better through being there all day."

Danette and Dineen were close in age, only fifteen months apart, so they were naturally each other's' first playmate, peer, and rival.

"We fought a lot but we were close," said Danette. "She would always be the one that got in trouble for this or that it would seem like."

When she was little, Danette remembers Dineen as a feisty young girl. She was always high energy and active.

"She literally would climb right up the wall. She would brace her feet between the doors and climb to the top. She was kind of a monkey."

Their baby brother Anthony, called AJ, was born more than six years after Dineen, so the girls spent a lot of time with just each other, outdoors, inventing games and making forts in the woods.

Ed Snyder also grew up in Cohocton with much less family support. He talks little about it. His uncle, Judge Ron Snyder, tried to fill in a little when Ed's dad was not around. He thought highly of his nephew and wanted to give him a male role model, however limited in scope.

"I used to stop to his house once in a while because I wanted him to have some kind of figure around," said Judge Snyder. "Then I kind of got away for quite a while, myself."

Chapter 3: Born into History

The Snyders stayed with family for a few weeks, and then, in May, Damien was born.

Soon they found a place of their own, a little house just up the street from Dineen's parents. They lived there for sixteen years.

"It was so nice being home with family and having family around to get to know the kids," Dineen reflected. "We were glad to have that opportunity."

Ed was on unemployment for a while, but then found a job working in one of the local fertilizer plants. He did many jobs in his ten years there: unloading rail cars, bagging fertilizer, scouting potato fields for pests, and recommending what sprays to use. Living in the picturesque Cohocton Valley with work and a large family may not have meant that the tragedy on the USS Iowa faded completely, but it did become more distant.

Though worlds apart, at the same time that the Snyder children were growing up, so was al Qaeda. Bin Laden, still operating from exile in the Sudan, emphasized to his fellow operatives the importance of hitting American targets in the Arabian Peninsula and in Somalia, even if it meant cooperating with Shiite groups like Hezbollah.

That next winter, in February of 1993, when Devin was 2½, Ramzi Yousef, an associate of Osama bin Laden, and others, bombed the New York World Trade Center for the first time. Six were killed and as many as a thousand injured. It was later revealed that their plan had been much larger, hoping that the explosion would topple one tower into the other. They had also planned other attacks on other New York City landmarks.[12] Bin Laden, focused on a similar strategy, was setting up al Qaeda training camps in Sudan.

At that time, Devin was still trying to grow hair. She was so fair-skinned and fine-haired that she was nearly bald until she was about three, when she finally started to show some little golden curls.

One sunny day later that year, in May 1993, Ed was busy with the endless springtime task of mowing the lawn. Dineen was inside, busy with the endless year-round task of doing dishes. The girls were playing quietly outside on the swings. It was a peaceful morning, Dineen thought. Everything was as it should be. Not long after that feeling of peace, Natasha came inside for a moment. Dineen didn't take much notice and Natasha went back outside to play. Soon after that, Devin came inside and Dineen found out why Natasha had come inside. She needed the scissors to give Devin her first haircut.

Dineen was very upset. Her father's birthday party was later that afternoon and the whole family would be there. She was embarrassed the whole day, but Devin beamed with pride at her and Natasha's handiwork.

That October, about two months after Devin's third birthday, eighteen American troops were killed when two Blackhawk helicopters were shot down in Mogadishu, Somalia by militiamen thought to be trained by bin Laden and al Qaeda. The Snyder children were occupied with what Halloween costume that they would wear.

"She was a tough kid sometimes," said Dineen, reflecting on Devin as a child. "She really was. She was good. But everything had to be her way. Even as a little girl she did not like people telling her what to do. She had a little bit of an attitude. She'd throw a temper tantrum and she would scream. She'd bang her head on the floor and look at you and scream again."

But Devin had a very sweet side, too.

"It was nothing for her to walk into her great-grandfather's house who lived two houses over and just crawl up on his lap," said Dineen. "She had such a loveable way about her."

Some of her abundant energy and aggression began to be focused into athletics. When Devin was 4, she ran in the Wayland Kids' Run sponsored by the local bank. It was early summer. The run was a quarter mile, around the track one time. A community event, it was assisted by the Wayland High School track team. Dineen signed up both Devin and Natasha, for fun, to get them out of the house and doing something active. Devin won first place, running it in her hiking boots.

"She was preparing for the Army even then," reflected Dineen, smiling about it years later.

Her uncle and aunt, Greg and Danette McInnis, were there to cheer her on.

"She was just a skinny girl taking big choppy strides," said Greg. "I just remember her destroying all the local kids. She was a third of the track ahead of everyone."

"I have very vivid memories of her doing that," said Danette. "She's got her little boots on she's so far ahead of everybody else."

When Devin was 5, two bombs exploded in a U.S.-Saudi National Guard training facility in Riyadh, Saudi Arabia. Seven were killed. Osama bin Laden, who had his Saudi citizenship revoked, was blamed.

In June of 1996, the Khobar Towers were bombed in Dharan, Saudi Arabia, an oil port near Bahrain that hosts the headquarters of the Saudi state-owned oil corporation, Aramco. Iran's state-funded terror group, Hezbollah, was responsible, though Al Qaeda took credit. Regardless, it was a victory for both brands of Islamic Fundamentalism. Nineteen were killed and 350 wounded. The blast was so big that it shattered all of the windows in a two-mile radius.[13]

When Devin was six, the Taliban took power in Afghanistan. Due to diplomatic and military pressure, Bin Laden was expelled from Sudan and al Qaeda then moved its base of operations to a familiar and remote location: Afghanistan. The Taliban used fear and force to conquer the people of Afghanistan, deploying the Department of Religious Observances, or religious police, to enforce their brand of strict sharia law. They carried whips, long sticks, and rifles to keep the populace in line. The list of prohibited activities included listening to or playing music, gambling, drinking alcohol, watching TV or movies, reading books other than the Koran, hanging portraits, flying kites, and keeping pet birds. Daily prayer was required, girls' schools were closed, and women were not allowed to work except as nurses, and only then in segregated hospitals. Women in Afghanistan bore most of the hardships under the Taliban. The *hijab*, or head-covering, was mandatory and "fashionable clothes" were outlawed. Those who wore "fashionable, ornamental, tight, and charming clothes... will be cursed... [and they] will be threatened, investigated, and severely punished," read one Taliban declaration.[14] The fundamentalist regime was so extreme that Iran even issued a statement accusing the Taliban of defaming Islam through their treatment of women.

At about that time, Devin was being empowered through her education. She was struggling in school, in both kindergarten and first grade because she had a small speech impediment and she pronounced the letter F as a B, so "frog" would be "brog" to little Devin. A speech therapist came to the house at that time to help her improve her speaking ability. The first thing that had to be done was to get Devin to slow down. Her eagerness contributed to her impediment. She was reminded to "turtle talk" rather than to "rabbit talk." This seemed to help her to scale down what she wished to communicate so that it could be formed in distinct sentences with clearly pronounced words.

In first grade, there was some concern because she was not reading yet. The teachers at her school talked about possibly retaining her. Dineen wanted to help. It was the era of what was known as the "whole language" approach. Special education teacher Jennifer Wolfanger helped by going against the orthodoxy and using old dusty phonics books and helping Devin to sound out discrete word parts. Early in her teaching career working with students with special needs, it was one of Miss Wolfanger's favorite success stories.

Late in the school year, Dineen quit her job at The Bank of Avoca, in a nearby town, and went into the school to see what kinds of activities she could do with Devin. With the guidance of the teachers, she spent all summer long that year working with Devin on reading all kinds of books. By October of the following school year, Devin was up to her grade's reading level.

Devin was also diagnosed with ADHD. A wild, outdoor, country girl unaccustomed to being bound by walls and large buildings, used to the wide open space of the valley that must have seemed to her young eyes like the whole world, she found it tiresome and difficult to sit at a desk in the small Cohocton first grade room.

Fortunately, soccer gave her an outlet for that unbridled energy. She started playing soccer on a small travel league.

At about that time, her older brother, Derek, moved out of the house. He was 16 and the confines of small town family life did not suit him, so he moved to Florida to work and live with older relatives. Derek and Devin were not that close, due to that age difference, but after her death, in an interview for WHAM 13 TV, he said that he admired her "feisty" quality.

"She had this strength about her that I couldn't explain," he said. "I didn't have it. I didn't know what it was. I don't try to explain things I don't know."

Perhaps that intangible quality was Devin's innate sense of fairness, and the fact that she would have no qualms expressing herself, loudly even, to anyone who was the perpetrator of an injustice.

"If she didn't agree with something or she didn't think something was right, she would go to the ends of the earth," said Dineen.

One day, while her brother Damien rode his bike on the sidewalk, Devin found a wooly bear caterpillar and held it in her hands. It was nice to pet, and fun to watch crawl up her arm. She decided to keep it and build a little house for it in the yard, so she scooped up some dirt into a pile, decorated it with sticks and leaves, and put the caterpillar on top to play.

Unable to resist, her brother Damien accelerated down the sidewalk toward her and ran over the caterpillar with his bike. This enraged Devin and she chased him down, tackled him off of his bike, and hit him. They were across the street and Dineen could hear the screaming. Justice had been served.

After years of physical work, Ed injured his back and needed a change, so he became a bus driver for the school district. All the while, he was trying to get a federal position in the boiler room of the Veterans Administration hospital two towns over, where he would get benefits and earn a pension. It took him thirteen years to get a job there.

"It's federal, so once someone is there, they don't leave until they retire."

In a way, the VA boiler room was like another homecoming for Ed. He was able to be around other veterans, and the workplace, for him, was reminiscent of being back on the USS Iowa.

"The first time I walked in there, an old navy BT [boiler technician] was in charge. We're walking through and he tells me all the stuff about the boilers and we're talking, talking, and that was my interview. He goes 'okay, when do you want to start?' So I started January third of 1998."

The same year, Dineen started working at the newly formed Wayland-Cohocton Central School. She had been a stay-at-home mom for several years, then took a job at a bank, then at a HeadStart program in Cohocton. She worked as a classroom aide for a few years and then transferred to the IT department and became computer lab monitor in the high school. She did that for 14 years before becoming the Superintendent's secretary.

"I'm a pencil pusher," she said later.

On Devin's 8th birthday, August 7, 1998, al Qaeda bombed the U.S. Embassies in Nairobi, Kenya and Dar es Salaam, Tanzania. The explosions killed over 200 people and wounded 5,000, leaving behind an all-too-familiar hellscape of rubble and exposed rebar skeletons of former office buildings, burning cars, smoke, and blood.[15] Osama bin Laden was later indicted on federal charges for the bombing.

By October of 1999, the UN agreed on sanctions against both the Taliban and al Qaeda. Seeing the danger in letting the two groups flourish any further, their funding, travel, and weapons trade were limited or frozen. Nevertheless, on October 12th, 2000, two suicide bombers ran a boat full of explosives into the USS Cole in Aden, Yemen, killing 17 sailors, among them several Navy women.

There is a photo of Devin from the following spring, on Easter of 2001. She is in a white dress with short sleeves. She stands in front of the altar at church, white taper candles in the background standing on both sides of her. She wears a straw hat with the brim turned up and holds a basket embroidered with flowers in both hands in front of her. She smiles.

That spring and summer, Devin played summer soccer again. In her bright orange jersey, she sprinted the green grass field kicking and chasing a ball so new that it shone in the sunlight. She sometimes scored the only goal of those games, booting the ball into the new nylon nets. At the same time, all throughout the highlands of Afghanistan, children kicked makeshift soccer balls, sometimes made out of bound rags, through goals marked in the sand.

On September 11th, 2001, Devin was 11 years old. She was in 6th grade at Wayland-Cohocton Middle School. Dineen was working in the High School Art Lab. She heard about the first plane hitting the first World Trade Center tower from someone in the hallway. Her first thought, like many of ours, was "Oh my gosh, pilot error."

"We all stood there watching it on TV and suddenly a second plane hit. I got chills," Dineen said. "It wasn't for another two hours or so that the government finally said that we were under attack. At that time, of course, I wanted to be down in the Middle School with the kids. I wanted to go get them."

Emily May, a friend of Devin's who is now a teacher at Wayland-Cohocton, was in Mr. Bondi's history class. The teachers had turned on the classroom TVs to see what was happening and then the second plane hit.

Another friend of Devin's, Meaghan Oas, was in another room.

"All of a sudden we were rushed out of the classroom across the hall and we sat there and watched it on TV," said Oas.

Everyone was shocked and didn't know what to do.

"That's when the announcement went over the speakers that all teachers should turn their TVs off," said May.

David Saxton, another friend and contemporary of Devin's, was in religion class at St. Joseph's Catholic School across town in Wayland. The school secretary came into the room and whispered something to the teacher. They exchanged a glance and then mildly shrugged.

"Some idiot flew their plane into a building," thought Dave when they first told the children.

When he looked at the adults, who seemed to be speaking in hushed voices, he knew something was not right. Later, at afterschool daycare at the public school, he and the other Catholic school children were asked not to tell the others. The school employees thought it would be best if the news came from their parents.

"The thing that blew my mind was the kids were all messing around and the adults are just kind of looking at each other really shell-shocked, but none of the kids noticed," said Saxton. "None of the kids noticed that the adults were just going through the motions of 'here's your bus, head home'. I remember they looked nervous. Really scared."

"They did not leave the TVs on in the middle school," said Dineen. "In the high school, everyone knew what was going on. You could just feel the dread."

Ed was still driving school bus during the day and had just returned home from his route. He turned on the TV and saw the flaming and smoking towers.

On September 12, the morning announcements began with a moment of silence. The mornings at school have begun that way ever since.

"She was very angry, I remember that," Dineen told WHAM 13 reporters years later, as they put together a special called "They Were Only 11," an in-depth look at Devin and local Marine Zach Smith. Both were from Western New York and both had their lives drastically altered that day. Both served their country and both were killed in action.

"She had painted a picture," said Dineen. "On it was a flag and the words 'United We Stand.'"

Television footage showed a photograph of Zach Smith climbing the fence to get a good look at what was then Ground Zero while on a visit to New York City.

It is impossible to think that this event did not have any effect on these two young people. The images of the falling towers, though not always present in their minds, became part of their childhoods. It is hard to conceive what that would be like, since many of us who remember it were adults when it happened, and though it changed our lives too, we had a stronger conception of what America was like before that event. These young people, such as Devin and Zach, may not have had that same sense of safety, that America could sustain such an attack. They may have felt unsafe and insecure in ways they had never felt before at the exact period of time in their lives when they were most impressionable.

Childhood psychologists have claimed for some time that the early adolescent period is when people begin to understand and develop their own abstract concepts. They also begin to logically test hypotheses.[16] In the social realm, the early adolescent period begins the process of distinct adult identity formation, wherein the young people find a role to play in society that fits with their own conception of self.[17]

"I can't speak for her but probably seeing everything unfolding on TV and watching these people's lives get taken, I think to her it was just she knew she wanted to do something about it," said Oas. "From that point on she wanted to join the service. From there on out I think it kind of changed her."

Not long after 9/11, the War in Afghanistan began. The Bush Administration openly embarked on a secular project, opposing the theocracies and sharia warlords there and proposing democratic rule. It began with a bombing campaign in October. Special Forces were deployed, and a relationship with anti-Taliban Afghan forces was forged.

By November, the Taliban was toppled. First Mazar-i-Sharif, then Kabul, then Jalalabad fell. Within a week, US and coalition forces had control over the capital and two major cities in the northeast of the country.

The Snyders celebrated Thanksgiving. Their family remembers few details about that time. What that likely means is that life was, in some ways, back to normal. The terrorists had changed a great deal of our national political conversations, but we, as a people, as a culture, were not ruined or toppled as they had hoped. The Snyders, like millions of others, ate turkey and gravy and cranberry sauce. Children teased each other and adults, perhaps, bickered over trivial matters. The TV was on. People dozed on their couches while Green Bay played Detroit, then Dallas played Denver.

By December 9th, the Taliban lost Kandahar, more or less ending their rule. Hamid Karzai was appointed as interim president. At the same time, the battle of Tora Bora raged on for weeks at the cave complex on the Pakistan border. The fortress, built into caves high in the mountains, was fully electrified, and powered by small hydroelectric dams on the mountain streams.[18] All remaining al Qaeda forces were destroyed or captured, but Osama bin Laden, the mastermind, escaped to Pakistan on horseback.

That Christmas, Devin and the other Snyder kids tore open presents in their pajamas. Dineen and Ed stumbled around the kitchen, making coffee. With steaming mugs in hand, they sat down to watch the tornado of wrapping paper. The tree jingled every time the dog brushed by it. The lights twinkled and the tinsel glowed.

In March of 2002, the US tried to regroup and Operation Anaconda began. The plan was to send a large enough force of Afghan soldiers, US soldiers, and International Special Forces to prevent Al Qaeda and Taliban from escaping into Pakistan, like they had at Tora Bora. Once the escape routes were sealed, soldiers worked to clear bunkers and confiscate weapons caches in the mountains. Later, it was reported that "bomb-making material, ammunition, terrorist manuals, medical equipment and supplies" were found in the caves.

The experience is chronicled in Andrew Exum's memoir *This Man's Army*. Exum, an Army Ranger, was deployed to NYC after 9/11 for disaster relief, and then deployed to Afghanistan.[19]

"It was the Wild West," he wrote, frequently revisiting that romantic metaphor, but it was also a war with incomprehensible violence and horror. "Eleven year olds we came across might be combatants just as dedicated to killing us as their fathers were," he noted.[20]

That same spring, eleven years old herself, Devin ran Modified Track and in July she played summer soccer.

Her soccer coach, Julie Martin, graduated from Cohocton High School, before the schools merged.

"I've known Dineen since we were little kids. My parents and her parents were friends. We used to play together when our parents would play cards."

Martin's graduating class at Cohocton High School was a group of 28.

"Mine was one of the bigger ones," she said with a chuckle.

Martin met Devin for the first time at a soccer camp. She had been coaching soccer for about ten years and had run many summer camps. Devin started out as one of the little ones at summer soccer camp and later was a counselor.

"Devin was always one of those spunky kids who wanted to be active," said Martin.

She played on the Modified/JV soccer team the next fall. It was 8th grade, the last year in the middle school before entering high school. For Devin, like many students, it was a time to start thinking about what she wanted to do with her life. Devin, ever focused on justice, wanted to be a lawyer.

This desire was influenced by her great uncle, Judge Ron Snyder. As he was Ed's role model, the children naturally looked up to him as well.

"I used to stop in for a friendly visit," he remembered. "All the kids would be there. Devin was always the one that stuck out in my mind as the girl with the energy. The one that just couldn't sit still. She was fun to be around."

At one point, Dineen went to work for Judge Snyder as court clerk. The court sessions were held at night in the hamlet of Atlanta, NY. The bench was smaller then, with a modest clerk's desk close by.

"Would you mind if Devin came down with me?" Dineen asked one night.

"No, not at all," replied Judge Snyder. He was pleased to have her there.

So for over a year, Devin would attend weekly court sessions, sitting right next to her mother.

"It was really neat," said Judge Snyder. "She took such an interest that I started giving her the old law books. Every time we did updates I'd give her the old ones. She would take those things and she was reading them. She was such a sweet kid."

She started looking into college and realized that law school was pretty expensive. So she started saving money in little piggy banks all over the house. Realizing perhaps that her savings method would never reach its goal, or perhaps simply shifting priorities, she decided that she wanted to go into the military. She was planning to go into the Navy, like her Dad.

Chapter 4: Horizons

Staying in Cohocton offered her few options, and like many ambitious young people, Devin's eyes were looking up toward the horizon. What was there? Just hills and the highway.

In some ways, Cohocton was the same as it had always been. Split rail fences marked property lines as they have since the land was first settled. There were well-groomed lawns, stone foundations, and white picket fences. In the fall, sunflowers held their final blooms. The leaves began to collect, drift down the surfaces of the dark creeks, and gather in yellow and orange piles along the roadside.

Judge Ron Snyder remembers when the state route was the only route, when 415, the winding, leisurely road, was the standard. Things started changing when the interstate was built. One small change he noticed, as a local judge, was an increase in speeding tickets.

"It got to a point where I was doing a hundred-fifty to a hundred-seventy-five cases a month. We still do well over a hundred a month, probably hundred-fifty, because of the interstate," said Judge Snyder.

He's seen many changes in his time. The old Cohocton Railroad Depot, which sits in disrepair like so many of the depots in Western New York towns, is a reminder of the heydays of the 20th century. The railroad used to connect Atlanta, Wayland, Perkinsville, then Dansville and up the Genesee Valley to Rochester. Passing by the spur that leads to Cohocton, the tracks led west, to Cleveland and then Chicago. Going south, the rail bed follows the Cohocton River south to Bath and Corning, then east to New York City. In its time, the Erie Railroad was the primary shipping route to and from the west. Today, the functioning rail only connects Cohocton, Atlanta, and Wayland, ending at Gunlocke, the wood furniture company. The little dead end rail spur is now often used for storing empty cars or engines needing refurbishing at the Alstom factory in nearby Hornell. But at one time, each of the little towns had its own railroad depot.

Judge Snyder remembers when the trains used to run at the depot in Atlanta, NY, one of three small hamlets in the Town of Cohocton. It was mostly freight and mail trains by then, few passengers, but he and his brother spent time there with their uncle, who was stationmaster. One of the conductors used to bring them candy when he would stop. Snyder would watch his uncle tap out messages in Morse code.

Agriculture was still a big driver of the local economy at the time. Judge Snyder's mother worked at the Birdseye Pea Vinery in Cohocton, on Pine Hill, where they hand-processed peas and beans along a conveyor. She was Devin Snyder's great-grandmother.

Boggs Manufacturing in Atlanta made potato graders, which sort the potato by size. They sold graders all over the country. Local farmers liked it because it could sort over 75 bushels per hour, reducing the need for human labor. Still, Cohocton and other towns in the area hosted migrant farm workers seasonally in order to harvest the potato crop.

The children attended school locally and the neighbors looked out for each other.

"Back when we were kids, we found things to do. We played kick the can and hide and seek," said Judge Snyder. "Now my grand-kids, if you don't find them, they're in their room on the computer playing games."

When Judge Snyder was young, the US was well into the post-WWII boom. People across the nation had decent paying jobs and were buying houses and cars, often with only one income in the family. The hamlets and the Village of Cohocton were different places then.

"They must have had five bars in the village of Cohocton," recalled Judge Snyder. "If you sit in one of those bars on Main Street it was nothing but truck after truck after truck that would drive through there. Tractor-trailers. They would come up Route 15 and turn at the light in Cohocton."

Judge Snyder remembers watching people come out of the bars, wondering if they would make it across all of that truck traffic.

"We used to laugh about it, but that was because the traffic was heavy even late at night," he said.

There were at least three or four small grocery stores spread in the three hamlets and one in the village.

"Most people didn't go out of town. We did our grocery shopping right here when we needed something," he said.

Then another big change came to the area: the supermarket.

"The big stores came about and all of a sudden everything started going downhill," said Judge Snyder.

The Cohoctonites, like most residents of small town America, could not then perceive the scope of the change that was to come. A contributing factor locally to this major global cultural and economic shift was the building of Interstate 390. As the population shifted to suburbia, development favored places that were easily accessible by car, along the highway, usually large flat expanses of what was once prime farmland where strip malls and shopping malls and parking lots could be built.

It happened over the course of twenty years or so, but people began selling their businesses and houses and moving elsewhere. Or when one of the pillars of the community fell, no one rose to take his or her place. Many people got out, moved to bigger towns, cities, suburbs, or wherever there were jobs and an easier, more "modern," way of life.

Of course, many of the towns wanted to be part of that development. The trend was toward consolidation and scaling up. It was either get with the program or die.

"Once 390 was in, it was almost like somebody flipped a switch. No traffic. That's when the motels went down, and the businesses went down, because there's no traffic," said Judge Snyder.

The Cohocton Creamery, opened before the turn of the century as the Wetmiller Creamery, closed down. Judge Snyder's brother, Theodore Snyder, grandfather of Devin Snyder, used to work there.

"They used to have a store and they used to have the mozzarella cheese they would put in the salt brine tank for testing and I would buy that because I always liked mine a little saltier," said

Judge Snyder, recalling the fresh mozzarella. "They knew that so when I'd go in there, I'd get a brick of that."

After a series of buyouts, the company was bought in 1968 by Polly-O, the string cheese manufacturers. In the 1980s, Polly-O was bought by Kraft Foods, a part of the Phillip-Morris Corporation. As greater profits were sought after, the plant was shut down and about a hundred people lost their jobs.[21]

The hamlet of North Cohocton once hosted a small but thriving business named Moore-Cottrell Subscription Agencies, which was a sort of middleman between publications and customers. They would sell subscriptions and then send them in bulk to magazines. The magazines would give them a bulk rate, they would take a cut, and the customer would get the magazines. They also had corporate accounts with Kodak Film and Xerox in Rochester, other companies as far as the west coast, as well as government accounts. Judge Ron Snyder worked there at one point.

"We had to do probably twenty-five million dollars a year, which was a lot. We employed most of the time a little over a hundred females. It was all clerks. All clerical stuff. At most there were seven or eight managers; I was a manager. Maybe another six or seven supervisors, the rest were clerks. At the peak we were a hundred-thirty."

Of course, it would be an understatement to say that the world of publishing has changed quite a bit. Some of those changes, as well as the great game of corporate acquisitions and mergers, meant that Moore-Cottrell would be bought out and then closed.

"I think all Upstate is just a death spiral," said Greg McInnis, Devin's uncle. "There are no jobs here."

"When I grew up all of the dads worked in town. All of our dads. They worked at the sawmill, the feed store, the fertilizer place, the grocery store, the carpet store."

"There was a bank in town. And a barbershop," said Devin's aunt, Danette McGinnis.

"We had a hardware store. It was thriving," said Greg.

Some of those changes have been cultural, not merely economic.

41

"There were as many churches as bars," said Danette.

"Presbyterian, Methodist, Catholic, two Lutheran," said Greg.

The general decay of the American small town can be seen by driving through any of the local communities. They're not totally lost. People do care, and it is those residents who hold the towns together. The yards in the village are well kept and the hedges are groomed. American flags and other patriotic memorabilia adorn neatly painted porches. A new garage is being built. However, right next door, a house looks abandoned. Down the street, large colonial homes line the road into the "downtown" area, where brick buildings loom like monuments of a more prosperous age. Carey's Grocery is on one side. The signage is simple but neat. Inside, the linoleum is scuffed by work boots. Across the street is a tanning salon, a furniture store, the public library, and the local historical society. Half a dozen trucks are lined up at the gas station on the other corner, awaiting repair.

One of the bright spots in Cohocton, literally, is the Cohocton Sports Complex, where football and soccer games are played at night under the lights. Standing in the fields there, one can see the long valley stretched out in a south-easterly direction, away, heading toward the coast. Not far from there, the Cohocton School still sits, a tan, Art Deco brick building built during the Works Progress Administration.

The Cohocton Sports Complex was the dream of several local residents, but specifically retired Physical Education teacher Ellsworth Tripp.

"This guy did it all," said Greg McInnis. "I don't know how he stayed married and had kids."

His ambition was to build sports fields in the middle of the nearby farm fields, sort of a "field of dreams" for football and soccer. However, Tripp was a teacher and he coached four or five sports each year, so he wouldn't be able to do it alone.

"It was a potato field. We'd go out and pick rocks," said Danette McGinnis, remembering the efforts of the students at Cohocton High School.

Early planning began in 1984 and by the end of the year, a scale model had been made. An architect who was a Cohocton native helped with the necessary plans. The Superintendent of the school was behind it and worked to navigate the bureaucracy in Albany for some of the funding. Other sources of funding included loans and fundraising campaigns.

"When you have a big vision, people get behind it," said Greg McInnis.

Once it was approved, in 1985, the project went ahead with an all-volunteer crew.

"From the day we started it was eleven days till they played their first soccer game on this field," said former Cohocton Mayor Tom Cox. "Eleven days. That was the type of volunteers we had here."

Cox, a long-time resident of Cohocton, recalled the effort:

"Men all went to work during the day but the women, sometimes there would be seventy women down there working putting the sand in the trenches and putting the conduit on the poles. There were only two paid people, two paid electricians on the whole thing down there. The other things were all volunteer so there wasn't any tax dollars in the place. There still isn't many tax dollars in the place. It's still run by the Booster club and the money from the gate and food stand finances what goes on down there. ...We got some pork barrel money to pay off most of the stuff because the most expensive thing down there was the bleachers, believe it or not... When the men got home we'd work till eleven at night and go to work the next day and come back. As we relieved the women, they would bring the food down. We had one front-end loader from the mill down here. We had a pickup truck that carried everything around. It was a 57 Chevy that only had reverse in it so every place we went we went in reverse. We had hay wagons on the back of tractors. It was probably the biggest red-neck project you ever saw in your life, but it got done."

Today, the children who play soccer and football there are likely the grandchildren of the volunteers who built it. More than a generation of people have sat on the bleachers and cheered on classmates and friends under the bright lights. On Friday nights, cold-handed fans sip steaming coffee or cocoa from Styrofoam cups, and nibble on French fries made from local potatoes. They huddle together wearing the colors of the home team, while the athletes on the grass fields below seek the glory of victory.

One of the icons of the Cohocton area is the maple tree, especially in the fall. The hand-painted sign on the road from the highway reads "Welcome to Cohocton, a Bicentennial Community," emphasizing the frontier heritage of the place, and its proud people. An image of an orange-leaved tree adorns the green sign. Symbolically speaking, the fall colors represent the end of the growing season, but also the harvest of the ripe fruit of the land for the coming months of winter. It is an emblem that celebrates the beauty of the present, but acknowledges that it does not last.

In late September and early October, the leaves begin to change, and the Cohocton community hosts the Fall Foliage Festival. Vendors from near and far line the streets with their canopies and crowds of people wander up and down to see the crafts, antiques, flea market wares, and artistry. The smell of fried dough is in the air. A few bushel baskets of bright red apples overflow on a green lawn near horses waiting to give wagon rides. There is a tractor pull, a car show, and a parade.

Two years later, the festival became better known because of a unique contest: tree sitting.[22] Contestants sat in the low branches of the maple trees by the school until they couldn't sit there anymore. Last person sitting wins. It would often go all weekend. Despite its popularity in the sixties and seventies, the tradition faded. People were allowed to use hammock chairs and finally the tree limbs were worn out. By 2009, the contest's final year, a 15-year old named David Lucas won while sitting with his feet up in a hammock chair and playing video games on a hand-held system.

The festival to this day generates money for scholarships and other special projects, like new picnic tables for the park. Attendance has dropped off to some extent.

"There was a time where we'd have a hundred thousand people through here in the weekend," said former Mayor Cox.

44

"Now we're probably down to fifty, sixty thousand. It's still pretty big."

"That's when everybody comes home from college," said Mikayla Sick, class of 2010. "Everybody sees each other. Everybody goes out and has a good time, all because of this little festival in our town. I don't think there's one person that doesn't look forward to Fall Foliage."

The weekend usually coincides with the school's homecoming, so it becomes a kind of reunion for graduates. Some, barely a month into their freshman year of college, drive home six hours to be there. Others make it back more regularly and others still never left. They all mix in the cold evening, under the lights of the Cohocton Sports Complex, while the football game goes on. Sometimes multiple games are going on at the same time and parents can be seen wandering back and forth between fields, trying to see both children play on homecoming night.

It is also time for the Spud Jug soccer game. Local schools compete for the right to paint their name on the side of an old earthenware jug.

At that time of year in Cohocton the corn is still green, but it is turning yellow. Rusty orange, yellow, and the bright red of maples, along with the persistent green of evergreens and stubborn oaks, which are the last to change, color the picturesque rolling hillsides. On a sunny day, when the sky is clear and blue, many motorcyclists are out, taking in the splendor along the curving roads. Red barns with stone foundations that have stood for a century stand above ponds encircled with white geese. It is a pastoral heaven.

These are the economic and elemental underpinnings of the small agricultural village in Steuben County called Cohocton, NY. It is a place of brilliant autumns, steep hills, narrow lakes, and ancient rivers. Though perhaps not fully conscious of them in their daily lives, these things make up both the physical and psychological landscape of Western New Yorkers. Wedged between Appalachia and the Great Lakes, hardened by winter, blessed with waterfalls, fishing streams, and hunting grounds, the people of this area enjoy local beauty even as they struggle to find opportunities in the global economic system. It is in this context that Devin Snyder's ancestors made a life and it is here that her young mind was filled with the love of country.

It is easy to assume that soldiers and citizens are patriotic because of some abstract love of country, some sense of duty to the nation of the United States of America. But there is something much deeper than that at work. It may not be that we love our nation as much as we love our *homeland*, and that when people enlist, they do so to serve the places that they love—the simple, yet beautiful village, the gently-flowing river, or the freshly-painted soccer fields in the center of a Coliseum of colorful leaves. Past joys are always in our hearts, even if we do not acknowledge them in the present.

Given this, it will be easier to see that Devin, and others like her, are at once deeply connected to a place and at the same time drawn to far off lands by the sense of duty to stand up for that place. Their love of home sends them away from home.

Chapter 5: Twiggy

Normal life carried on. The Snyder siblings maintained their rivalry religiously. The girls' arguments sometimes got physical.

"We were arguing in the living room at our old house and she tried to chase me up the stairs and then instead of turning the corner at the top of the stairs her arm went straight through the window," remembered Natasha Snyder.

Luckily, no one was injured. Ed, angered at the broken window, made it known that they would have to settle down. But it wouldn't be the last time that the girls would fight.

"She definitely had a temper and you wanted to get out of her way when she was mad," said Natasha.

Another fall passed, another Christmas, and another winter. This was the period of the lead up to the Iraq War. News reports swirled with UN inspectors and the fear of WMDs.

By late winter of 2003, on March 20th, the Iraq war began. The bombing of Baghdad was televised live on CNN. The shock and awe campaign was called a "decapitation attack" because it was aimed at Saddam Hussein and the top Iraqi leadership. Forty Tomahawk cruise missiles were among the weapons used.

Of course, Saddam was not harmed and later appeared on camera denouncing the attacks, calling us "criminal Zionists." He called for resistance saying, "Draw your sword" to any of the "dignified people" of Iraq. He ended his speech, according to CNN, by saying "Long live jihad and long live Palestine."[23]

The war went on. No WMDs were found and there was a general feeling of having been betrayed by the Bush Administration, despite high approval ratings after 9/11.

Unaware of, or at least undeterred by any of this, Devin was moved up to the Varsity Track team. She was very young, but some of the older girls took her under their wings and made her feel at home.

"When we first saw her, we were like 'That girl is so scrawny,'" said Emily May. "But Devin was the toughest, hardest-working girl I have ever met in my life. We did not give her enough credit at first. I just think that girl would teach girls that it's okay to be confident no matter what you look like."

On May 1, 2003, US Secretary of Defense Donald Rumsfeld announced the end of combat operations in Afghanistan.[24] On May 2, President George W. Bush stood in front of the now famously ironic "Mission Accomplished" banner on the USS Abraham Lincoln aircraft carrier and declared "major combat operations in Iraq have ended."[25] The focus of both theaters in the War on Terror would move to security and reconstruction.

Devin's focus was on running distance events for the Wayland-Cohocton Girls Track Team. Her coach, Mr. Jeff Englert, who coached Girls Track for 25 years, started in the early nineties with only nine girls and built the program up over the years.

"The first few years were tough, but I decided to make it work," said Coach Englert.

Throughout the course of his career, he had 209 wins, 72 losses, 7 NYS Section V Championships, 8 Coach of the Year Awards, and 3 league championships.

"After 1995 I never had a losing season," he said.

His secret, he said, was to recruit the best kids. When asked what that meant he said that the best kids are the ones who respond well to coaching, and who stay out of trouble and are generally positive individuals.

"From the mid-nineties on, I had 40 or more kids on the team every year. I think that's because I see in them something that they don't see, something special."

Englert, known to be a headstrong but excellent coach, said that he treats everyone the same.

"Some people will say that I treat everyone hard, but you get what you get," he said. "I push everyone and want everyone to improve."

Of course, that's where he and Devin sometimes "knocked heads," he said.

"I knew the buttons to push with Devin. You had to challenge her. If you told her she couldn't do something, then she would fight to prove you wrong," said Englert.

The assistant coach was Mr. Saxton, who specialized in coaching distance runners.

"Mr. Saxton was a great runner so he really knew how to train us and push us to the limits in a good way to where I have never been in better shape, and I play college soccer!" said Emily May. "I was in better shape when Saxton was coaching me than any other place I've ever played. He was just a good guy genuinely caring about us and wanting us to do our best."

The result: Devin had the steeplechase record in the first few years.

The season progressed and the girls participated in fundraisers so they could go on a trip to Florida for training. It was really more of a road trip and team-building exercise, but it was entirely paid for by their hard work.

"So the first year, she got moved up in eighth grade, and Englert's rule was that if you're an eighth grader, you don't get to go on the Florida trip," said Emily May. "This was a rule. I don't know why, but... He let her come in eighth grade. We took her under our wing and she just had a blast."

When they arrived, they did drills and scrimmaged during the day. At night, the girls went out to eat and saw local attractions.

One night, the girls were to go out to dinner. For some young people in rural New York, an outing like that might be the first time they had ever been to an expensive restaurant. Some of the older girls, noticing her tomboyish appearance, decided to dress Devin up "as a girl." Nike shorts or sweatpants and other athletic gear were regular features of her wardrobe. She needed to wear a skirt and a blouse, perhaps some nice shoes, in order to look respectable for dinner.

"I didn't bring clothes like that," admitted Devin. Neither did Alyssa Englert, Jeff's daughter who was also on the varsity team at a young age.

So May and the other girls borrowed or bought clothes. They made Devin wear a dress and heels, and make-up, out to dinner. They dressed Alyssa up as well. Devin stumbled awkwardly in the heels and because of her thin frame and skinny legs, she was nicknamed Twiggy. It stuck.

In August, NATO forces took over security in Afghanistan. The operation was dubbed "Enduring Freedom." Its mission was "to enable the Afghan government to provide effective security across the country and develop new Afghan security forces to ensure Afghanistan would never again become a safe haven for terrorists."

Another fall came and went with Devin playing on the JV soccer team, another holiday season, and another winter.

Natasha had a car at that time and began driving Devin around.

"I tried to show off in front of friends and I backed right into a fire hydrant," said Natasha.

After inspecting the massive scratch on the bumper, Natasha worriedly drove them home. Devin rushed inside.

"Mom, guess what Natasha just did!" said Devin.

In January of 2004, the constitution of Afghanistan was written, beginning democratic rule. Similar to the American system, the new constitution provided for three branches of government, due process, and many civil rights, such as freedom of expression, assembly, and even religion, to an extent. Though other religions are allowed to practice their faiths, Islam is still the official religion, and the state that was set up is an Islamic Republic, so men and especially women were still expected to follow Islamic traditions.[26]

In March, 191 Spanish civilians were killed and over 1,800 were injured when a series of backpack bombs exploded on four different trains in Madrid during the morning commute. The group that was responsible claimed al Qaeda affiliation.

In Afghanistan, people struggled to register to vote as Taliban resistance increased, targeting voter registration centers and those holding registration cards.[27] The United Nations Assistance Mission in Afghanistan (UNAMA), formed to help "international civilian efforts in assisting Afghanistan, guided by the principle of reinforcing

Afghan sovereignty, leadership and ownership," operated about 1,600 registration centers, and registered about 10.5 million voters, 42% of whom were women.[28]

The following year, in March of 2005, Devin won the Run for Shamrocks 5K, a YMCA fundraiser. It was beginning to be clear that in running, she was a formidable opponent.

While businesses failed or closed in Cohocton and while the economy stagnated, on the hills a new resource was discovered: wind. Standing high over the valley, above the Larrowe House, which was converted into the village municipal building, over the forested hills and fields of corn and soybeans, white wind turbines began turning in the blue sky.

The Dutch Hill/Cohocton Wind Farm consists of 50 turbines capable of producing 2,500 kW each.[29] The project, developed by First Wind, was very controversial for local people, at times even driving families apart.

One landowner who was against the development was Greg McInnis, Devin's uncle.

"You do not want one near your house," said Greg.

He and his family live on an idyllic and well-groomed rural property. Multiple outbuildings with matching paint surround the beautiful, wood-adorned home, which sits overlooking a pond. A forested hill behind the pond and the quiet serenity of this pastoral life is oddly juxtaposed with a very industrial sound. It is not quite a grinding sound, but something like the drone of gears turning.

"In the winter time you can hear it in the house," said Greg.

Far from being beautiful or charming to Greg, he was very distraught when they went up.

"I couldn't go on my land for two years. I was sick. I grew up here. I hunted here. I love the land. We own two-hundred acres."

Greg and Danette moved back to the area after a few years away and developed the site of their property, built the house and all of the outbuildings, dug the pond, and created their own hillside Eden.

When the wind turbines went up, one was constructed just on the other side of their property line. They didn't know about it until construction began.

Though the McInnis family might have felt betrayed by the building of the windmills, for Town of Cohocton Supervisor Jack Zigenfus, the project was the signature achievement of his time in public office.

"That is a two-hundred-sixty million dollar project which generates millions of dollars in revenues to the town over the years. It generates money to the school district and to the county."

Still, other residents, like Greg McInnis, remain skeptical about the deal.

"It's a real savior," said Greg sarcastically. "It's eleven million dollars over a twenty year period and the present value of that makes it about... four and a half to five-million today..."

"My biggest thing was where is the next dollar going to come from?" said Zigenfus. "Are you going to tax the farmers out of business or are you going to get an industry in that is going to generate millions of dollars?"

With few other prospects on the horizon, Supervisor Zigenfus decided that he was going to do whatever he could to bring the wind farm to Cohocton. He was met with strong resistance.

"They created a group called the Cohocton Wind Watch made up of a bunch of people that lived here but there were also many outsiders who had nothing to do with Cohocton that kind of jumped on the bandwagon...I'd have a meeting down here at the town hall with people holding up signs saying 'Communism at work'. I remember having people stop in front of my house and at the time my kids were little. I actually had a couple people arrested. I wasn't going to back down."

Zigenfus stands by his decision.

"The first year alone we took in a million dollars. That's unheard of. To me, I'd do it again," he said.

During that summer of controversy, Devin worked at Lawrence Parks Recreation Area in Cohocton as a counselor in the summer program for younger children. The park hosts a pool, a basketball court, volleyball court, and a playground. It is a sort of outdoor YMCA for rural children. A bridge in the park spans the Cohocton River and one of the pavilions are now named in Devin's honor.

Co-worker and friend Tyler Austin grew up in Cohocton with Devin. He remembers it being safe and enjoyable. Kids would be out late at night in the village or at the soccer fields without their parents worrying.

"Wayland and Cohocton are very close-knit communities," said Austin. "Whenever you go back it's like you never left. Everybody knows everybody. I don't miss the small town at all, but I miss the small town."

Tyler and Devin themselves were products of the summer program at Lawrence Parks Recreation Area, and working there brought them closer together. Tyler was a lifeguard at the pool. Devin worked as a counselor.

"It was a lot of fun," said Austin. "She brought life to everybody really. She made everybody smile."

Dineen had been hired to work as the coordinator of the summer program the previous year and Devin attended as a volunteer the first year. Dineen encouraged Tyler to get his lifeguard certificate. Natasha was working as a lifeguard and swim instructor. Damien was young enough to attend the program still.

"We were all in the same area at the swimming pool," remembered Natasha fondly.

On the back road between Cohocton and Atlanta, the park sits in a strange location: on a few acres in the midst of rolling hills of farm fields. It is an oasis in the corn.

"The program is two-fold," said Jack Zigenfus, former Town Supervisor. "One is a swimming program. The other is recreation. My big thing about the park is this: the park costs us. We lose tens of thousands of dollars a year on that park, but if you teach one kid to swim and prevent one kid from drowning, it is worth it."

Because of some of the tax revenue from the wind turbines, major restorations and improvements were made at the park.

"We were able to put a lot of money into the pools, electrical systems, filters; we put a brand new filter system in and that was thirty-five thousand dollars alone," said Zigenfus.

For three summers in a row, Devin worked with local children. Busses brought students from Cohocton and Atlanta for the afternoon. They would make crafts, play sports and games, and swim. Dineen managed the schedules of the counselors and lifeguards, and set up lesson schedules. Devin had a gift for engaging students who were down.

"If there was a kid that had a problem or just needed that one-on-one, she was drawn to them," said Dineen.

Working at the park also represented an opportunity for Ed and Dineen to teach Devin their values.

"She knew if she wanted something she had to work hard for it because we were never rich by any means," said Ed.

This later translated into a work ethic even at home.

"It was nothing for her to get up from the dinner table and start doing dishes or vacuum the floor or go get the dusting spray and dust the end tables," said Dineen. "She just knew to automatically pick up and help out."

On July 7th, Islamic Extremists set off three different bombs in the London Underground and one on a double-decker bus. Fifty-two people were killed and over 700 were injured. The perpetrators were found to be independent terrorist cells, but admirers of Bin Laden and others like him.[30] Two weeks later, another coordinated bombing failed at four additional transportation locations.

On September 18th, Afghans voted for their national congress and local councils. It was the first time women were allowed to vote and the first time that women were elected to public office in the new Islamic Republic.

In the fall of 10th grade, Devin continued to play soccer. Her parents attended most of the games, and sometimes kept score. Tyler Austin lived nearby the soccer fields and would sit with them inside the press box. He played Boys Soccer until he was hurt his senior year.

"I was always up in the press box with her parents. They would always be running the scoreboard and everything. Once I graduated I'd go over and watch when Damian was playing, her little brother. So boys games, girl games, I was always over there helping her parents with the scoreboards," said Austin.

In October, around the time of that year's Fall Foliage Festival and Spud Jug soccer game, Hamid Karzai was elected as President of Afghanistan. The democratically elected government issued a joint declaration with the United States to help "organize, train, equip, and sustain Afghan security forces," as well as to "encourage and facilitate involvement of U.S. businesses in ventures that accelerate the development of Afghan firms and the private sector."[31]

Around that time, Devin was discovering that her feisty temper could have negative consequences. Dineen tells the story of a time when she and Devin and Damien stopped at Carey's Grocery to get coffee before school. Damien had recently had a couple of moles removed from his face. As the three were waiting in line, Devin was not moving forward for their turn to pay and Damien put his hand on her back and pushed her ahead. Devin, irritated by her brother, turned around and punched him in the face. The stitching from the mole removal broke open and blood streamed everywhere.

"The lady at the register went and got us paper towels and we cleaned it up, but we had to take him to the emergency room," recalled Dineen.

"She had a very, very short fuse," said Damien.

According to Dineen, the silver lining was that she knew she had to learn self-control through that experience.

"She felt horrible," said Dineen.

The conflict between teenagers was not limited to Devin and Damien. Sometimes fights would erupt between the girls that were even more rowdy than the earlier ones.

"I never stuck around for it though," said Damien. "Normally I was on my way out the door. They were getting real vulgar with each other and I just left."

"We fought a lot," said Natasha. "We shared a room so we were always fighting, but we were still very close. She could talk to me about anything; I could talk to her about anything. We both knew it... Our relationship never really changed."

In the spring of 2006, Devin ran track again and she and Natasha were on the same team.

"We were always in indoor and outdoor track together but we were never together because I did sprint and she did long distance," said Natasha. "I mean, we were always together in one way, shape, or form. I was trying to make it to all of her soccer games and she would try to make it to all of my swim meets. She was there when I broke the record for 500 free-style."

That spring, the girls went on the track trip to Florida again. Devin was quickly becoming one of the leaders of the team.

"I think my dad does a good job of reading individuals and coaching them based on what's best for them," said Alyssa Englert. "He knew the times that he had to yell at her and he knew the times that he had to bring her in, and give her a hug, a pat on the back, say 'You're doing fine. Keep it up. Just keep working hard and you're going to be fine.'"

Coach Englert focused on what was best for the team, so his emphasis was on the greater good.

"My dad is good at not pointing fingers and blaming," said Alyssa, "not saying 'you need to be better' but 'your team needs you to be better'... I think he was able to do that with Devin and I think that motivated Devin because she didn't want to let the team down. So that's what drove her and my dad figured that out quickly and used that as a tool to make her perform better."

The Florida trip went smoothly. The school year was coming to a close and summer vacation was just around the corner.

On June 7th, 2006, Abu Musab al-Zarqawi, leader of al Qaeda in Iraq was killed in a US airstrike.

In late June, Natasha graduated from Wayland-Cohocton High School. She enlisted in the Navy, like her dad.

"Quite honestly, the kids followed Ed because they did have a lot of respect for him," said Dineen. "Natasha wanted to follow her dad in the worst way going into the Navy. Devin, she wanted something challenging and was not going to follow her sister, as much as she wanted to follow her dad. She wanted something more. That led her to the Army."

In July, the opposition in Afghanistan increased greatly. Insurgents were perhaps emboldened by their outrage at the elections and many more of the Afghan people began to support them as news of civilian deaths by US drone strikes spread.

That summer, Devin attended soccer camp at Houghton College, a rural Christian college in New York. She and Emily May decided to room together. Their newfound freedom in a college dorm led them to experiment with makeup.

"This one time," remembered Emily May, "I don't know what we were thinking; we decided to dress up very silly. We were putting creepy makeup on and our hair was in pigtails and we didn't plan on anyone seeing us."

Just then, the fire alarm went off and they had to go downstairs and outside.

"We were just so embarrassed."

Amid the strange looks from nearly everyone at the camp, Devin laughed it off.

"Oh my God, I can't believe we're outside in this," said May.

"Don't be embarrassed!" said Devin, and she started dancing around as they waited to return to their dorm rooms. It was then that they really know that Devin was special. She didn't care what people thought of her.

"She just rocked it," said May. "We just would always have a great time and we'd always be laughing."

Her junior year was much like her other years in high school. In the fall, Devin played soccer in the Spud Jug Classic under the lights during Fall Foliage. A big crowd was there to cheer them on.

"During the day we would go around and eat the fried food, which was a terrible idea, but we'd do that all day," said May. "Then we met on the field at night. It was really fun."

School days were a mix of classwork and socialization.

"Seems like every time you would walk into a room a rubber band would come across the room at you or something just to catch you off guard," remembered Tyler Austin.

"I was in her mother's room constantly and anytime you'd walk into that room she was sitting there… She was always just the goofy one… The way she stood. I don't know what to call it but it was just very awkward the way she stood."

On November 5, Saddam Hussein was executed by hanging. Video leaked on the internet shows that, in addition to being taunted by his captors, Hussein's final prayer was interrupted as the trapdoor was released, causing outrage among Sunni Muslims against the majority Shia government.[32]

In the spring, Devin ran Varsity Track again. Coach Englert continued to push her. Every once in a while he'd have to let her know that he expected more of her. Maybe during a practice, he would tell her "Well, maybe that's all you got," then walk away. She wouldn't like that, and at the next meet she would be sure to show him that she could do more.

"And I always knew she could," said Coach Englert.

"She was funny," said Alyssa Englert. "She was a good leader in the sense that she was able to lead by example. She always had a smile on her face even when we were dying from workouts in the middle of track season in the beating sun and my dad's yelling at us to do something again she's like 'Come on guys! Let's go beat Englert's workouts.' So that was my first impression of Devin."

Her competitive streak was developing and maturing as the season went on.

"The thing about Devin was that she was very competitive, and I wanted that to come out more," remembered Coach Englert. "In soccer, it is more of a team sport, so that is easier to muster, but track is very much an individual sport, so you have to push yourself.

If she wasn't doing that I would let her know, and she didn't always like me for that. But a day or two later we would be friends again."

But Englert was not one to point out only the girls' weaknesses. Like a good coach should, he offered encouragement as well. He gave out suckers to anyone who achieved a personal record.

"It might seem like a silly thing," he said, "but to those girls, the suckers were like gold rings."

He also helped Devin maintain her confidence in the early years. If she had a bad race, or was just in pain due to the training and the changes that a young woman's body goes through at that time in her life, he would help her keep her hopes up.

"I don't know what's wrong with me," she would say.

"You gotta run through it," he would say.

Or there might be races that just didn't go her way. Seeing that she was upset, he would talk her through it.

"What happened?"

"I just don't have it."

"Yes, you do. You just have to work through it. You're a young woman."

She would have support from the other girls on the team, who were beginning to call themselves "track sisters," but sometimes the support would manifest in strange ways.

"So when you saw one of your sisters in the hall you'd try to embarrass the person in the middle of the hallway or make them laugh or do something funny or I don't know run up and give them a hug or something like that. So with Devin it was like that," remembered Alyssa Englert.

Other times, Devin would be the voice of support.

"I guess it just goes back to her confidence," said Emily May. "All of the time I might be down about something she would always come to me and be like 'Why? You can do it. If I can do it you can do it.' Before races she was always determined."

"I think she liked to win," remembered May. "Not in a cocky way, but I think she likes to always beat herself. In track she always wanted to beat her personal best time and I think that was easier to motivate her because she wanted to beat herself more than anything."

As she was one of the upperclassmen on the team, Devin became a role model for other girls. Mikayla Sick, nicknamed Kaya, was pulled up to Varsity Girls Track in her eighth grade year, just as Devin had. But now, the younger girls looked up to her.

"She was kind of like a big sister," said Mikayla. "I was kind of put under her and Emily May's wings. I was supposed to do everything they did."

She was placed in many of the distance events with Devin, and grew to know her well.

"I did every single track event she did except for steeple chase," said Mikayla. "That just shows her perseverance right there, being able to do steeple chase. I did the 400 hurdles because that's what Devin did, I did the 400 because that's what Devin did. I did the 4x4 relay because Devin was on it, I did the 4x8 relay because Devin was on it. Anything she did I just wanted to do. I wanted to be. I wanted to show her that I could be her and fit in with her all the time… It was a good goal to have."

"She would call me her big sister and stuff when we were younger," said Emily May. "She always found ways to get in trouble in track. It'd be like 'where did Kaya go now?' Devin and her and I were close."

"Kaya looked up to Devin," said Dineen. "She had a lot of respect for her, I know."

"If you look at those two together, they look like twins," said Ed.

"They look like sisters," said Dineen. "People had mistaken them for sisters before."

As the senior girls were coming to the end of their time in high school, they asked Devin what her plans might be for the future.

"I remember we asked her one day because we were already about to head to college," said May. "I wanted to be a teacher. Cait (another friend on the team) wanted to be in health. Sometimes she wouldn't know but most of the time it was some type of military because of her dad. I think she felt strongly about that."

That June, Tyler and Emily graduated, along with other good friends. Tyler went to a local community college and majored in Sports Studies. Emily studied education.

That summer of 2007, Devin was one of the first groups of soccer players who went on a retreat to a place in Springwater, New York called "Punky Hollow," a lodge and sprawling rural property belonging to Gene Miller, the owner of Rochester Steel, for team building and a preseason workout. After a few years, Miller generously paid to have trees cleared and an area bulldozed so that there was a full-sized soccer field for the girls to play on.

Martin, for the first couple of years, when Devin was there, took the soon-to-be senior girls on a hike through the woods. As they hiked, she talked to them about the importance of having the girls on the team, the significance of sports (especially soccer) in their lives, and asked the girls to tell them what soccer meant to them.

"I like that coach Martin took us and took away the teams' cellphones so we had each other pretty much," remembered Alyssa Englert. "And outside of practicing once or twice a day we went on hikes and had campfires and just kind of had girl pillow talks and stuff. We were all in one big giant room and there were tons of bunk beds. So we all slept in the same room."

Often times the subject of their future plans would come up. Martin, a firm believer in the positive impact of sports on the lives of young people, tried to help the girls understand how their mental and physical toughness would help them meet their goals.

On that ritual walk just before Devin's senior year, Devin knew that she was going into the Army and spoke excitedly about entering into the military police. She was proud to carry on the family tradition and serve like her father and sister did before her, but in her own way.

"She didn't want to follow in the exact same footsteps that I did," said Natasha. "She wanted to create her own path and that's what she did."

"I know she did it for the right reasons," reflected David Saxton, who was also on the track team. "I know afterward a lot of people said that she did talk about it a lot but I think she didn't go too crazy with telling people that's what she wanted to do because I don't think she wanted people to make her second-guess herself."

It was then that she started to become more like her adult self.

Even her peers began to notice.

"I got to see her grow over the years in school," said May. "She was just this confident girl and she didn't take crap from anyone. She just knew who she was and what she wanted in the world."

"She always wanted to better herself," remembered Tyler Austin. "Was always working on soccer or working on school. Always wanted to be better. Other than that she was courageous, obviously. When she said she was going into the army it hit hard, but she always wanted to help everybody. That's just who she was. I'm sure her family was an influence with their history in the military, but she wanted to be right in the action. She wanted to be the one helping, doing the most."

When she finally got accepted into the Army, she came to practice with her Army sweatshirt on.

"She was proud as could be," said Martin.

"Even though she was very good at track and very successful, I think that she loved soccer the most," said Martin. "It was her passion."

"Devin definitely had the passion for it," said May.

"Everything was a mission to her," said Mikayla Sick. "Everything she did was full force. She never half-assed anything. She was all in or not at all."

Even on the soccer field, Devin was a leader. She played forward or midfield because she distributed the ball well.

"She was very unselfish," Martin remembered.

"She had a lot of assists," recalled her brother Damien.

There were times, even in soccer, when her temper would get the best of her.

"Obviously everyone talks trash and everybody gets violent, especially on a soccer field," said Damien. "Somebody chopped one of her friends and she went after that person and she apparently ended up breaking her leg or arm or something… I'm not going to say as revenge but it happened."

Most of the time, she would channel that anger into motivation. She took practices very seriously and if there were times when the other girls were goofing around, she would get them back on track.

"She wanted to win," said Martin. "It was important to her."

"I wouldn't let my sister drive me to school," remembered Mikayla Sick. "I had to go to school with Devin, who was way cooler, you know? We mainly just laughed at music and sang at the absolute top of our lungs."

After school, Devin and Mikayla would drive around or play mini golf badly on purpose. Devin would offer her advice about how to navigate the drama of high school.

"She always tried to shelter me I think from anything bad going on," said Mikayla. "She'd tell me 'Don't worry about those girls because I'm the one that matters, I'm going to be there for you no matter what… Devin always gave me advice that you don't need a hundred friends, you need three great friends. You don't need to be the most popular in the school as long as you have a couple really good friends. That's what you'll remember. Those friends will get you through the harsh times."

Devin used the winter to stay in shape for track in the spring. Fortunate enough to attend one of the few rural schools with an indoor track, Devin ran distance that winter in the Wayland-Cohocton Fieldhouse. Indoor track gave her another outlet for her energy and gave her the opportunity to make other good friends.

Meaghan Oas was on the team with her and was also in her graduating class.

"We were the same year. Twelfth period we would have government and economics with Mr. K and Mr. Robinson and she and I were notorious for getting out of class. One of us saying we were going to the bathroom, one of us saying we were going to our lockers and wandering the halls. That was our thing senior year."

Oas ran indoor track mostly to be social, hang out with friends, and meet people.

"It was more fun than competitive for me," she said. "There was no way I could keep up with her and half the time I wouldn't even try."

The team would take long bus trips north to Rochester Institute of Technology where some of the meets were held. Returning late, Meaghan and Devin excelled at goofing off.

"There was one track meet we got back to school and the girl's locker room down in the field house was locked. The only one that was open was the guy's. We had to go to the bathroom and the coach didn't want to go all the way over and unlock the door so we just went in the men's. We went in the men's locker room and just for the fun of it we tried to go to the bathroom in a urinal. It turned into pure laughter and giggling and it was pretty much impossible."

"In the hallways we would do stupid stuff," remembered Oas. "It was cool to try to trip yourself or trip each other while walking down the hallway. That was one of the things. Devin, with her long legs, it was so easy to trip her. So we would trip her and everyone would laugh and she had this laugh that was just contagious."

That spring was Devin's last season of track. She was a senior and became a captain of the team. Inspired by Sam Parker's motivational book *212: The Extra Degree*, Devin and Dineen designed t-shirts for the girls with 212° on the back. She took her leadership role very seriously and knew that she always needed to be at her best, and to lead by example.

"People had a natural respect for her. The girls respected and followed her," said Coach Englert.

Mikayla Sick, unlike Devin, did not adapt to Coach Englert's authoritative style.

"I always remember Devin always being like 'If he said something let it go. Be respectful and let it go. You can talk to me about it but don't talk to him about it.'"

Still, as a senior nearing graduation, Devin was not above breaking some rules.

"After school, we would jump into Devin's jeep as fast as we could," remembers Mikayla, "We'd drive to the Food Mart and get popsicles, put them in a cooler, and sometimes when we went for a run with the distance team, we would go and eat the popsicles instead of run."

That spring break, the Girls' Track Team went on their bi-annual trip to Florida to compete and train. In one of the track meets, the girls nearly won, even though they had only been practicing for a few weeks. They knew that they had the talent that year. It was only a matter of wanting to succeed.

"I got to spend the night with the girl I looked up to the most and that was the first time we really started to connect," said Mikayla. "I was supposed to stay with her and make sure that I was being good because I was new. I just thought I was so lucky because I got to hang out with her. I got to do everything with her on the trip. I followed her to Old-Town. We bought stuff. We did the scavenger hunt together. No matter what, I wanted to keep up with her."

During the trip, the girls went to a mall to eat and go shopping. Several of the girls found the mall security to be pretty weak, so they stole some clothing and jewelry. Devin saw what was happening at the mall, but didn't say anything at the time.

When Devin returned from the trip, her behavior was noticeably different. She was not eating much, not sleeping, and seemed to be down in general. Dineen asked her what was going on. She was conflicted, she told her mom. She didn't want to go against her track sisters, but she had to tell the truth.

"I think Devin might have confronted one of them and said 'look you need either to turn yourself in or I'm going to turn you in,'" remembered Alyssa Englert. "I'm pretty sure that's what happened. She was trying to do the right thing and make them hold themselves accountable for what they did. And when they didn't, she did."

At school, when they returned, Coach Englert was heading to the middle school gym and Dineen caught him in the hall.

"I have to walk you to your gym," she said. "Devin's waiting for you."

Coach Englert was somewhat confused, but agreed. He suspected something was wrong, but hoped that it was not something wrong with Devin.

He walked in, and Devin was there, nervous and pacing.

"Something has been bothering me since we got back from Florida. I haven't been able to sleep. I have too much respect for you and Mr. Saxton to keep it from you."

"Well, lay it on me, girl," he said, trying to encourage her. "Let's get it out and deal with it."

"Mr. Englert, that day you took us to the mall, a bunch of girls stole. They robbed that place blind. We told them to knock it off, but they didn't listen."

"Are you kidding me?" said Mr. Englert. "How many people know about this?"

"I don't want to tell on the other girls, but this is wrong. I feel just as guilty because I didn't say anything before."

Dineen was crying.

"Thank you. Let's keep this between us for now."

Whatever love-hate relationship that existed between Coach Englert and Devin before was gone. Now, they had a much closer relationship. He knew he could trust her.

Then she gave him a list of all the girls who were involved.

"There's going to be a shake up this week, but don't worry about it because we are still going to win," he told her.

He decided to check the story and called down another senior. She told him that when he and his wife were waiting for girls to come out of the stores, many of them lied. Englert was no fool, he knew that kids would sometimes steal, so he "innocently" asked the girls what they bought and tried to read their reactions, but the girls who stole showed them and didn't show any guilt.

Mr. Englert called a meeting and told 57 parents what had happened and ten girls were kicked off of the team.

"Some of the girls deserved it, but I also lost some great girls because of that, some young girls who just got caught up in it," said Englert.

"I was one of the girls that was young and I was told to take things from the store because it was my initiation," said Mikayla Sick. "When Devin found out she was so upset with me. I felt more disappointment from her than anger. She's the kind that if you disappoint it's ten times worse than making her mad. That broke my heart but of course she's forgiving. She said 'Learn from it, don't do it again. I understand that it's hard' and she got mad at the other upperclassmen for saying that was initiation. So she was disappointed and that made me feel awful, of course."

Then Coach Englert called all of the stores, found out what was missing, and told the girls they had to send everything back.

Later, Devin owned up to the fact that she was the one who told.

"I think that was the only time that people were on the outs with her," said David Saxton.

At a meet not long after, the girls were noticeably down. On the bus, Englert told them that they would move on and win anyway. He left the bus for a moment and could hear Devin and the other senior girls at the back of the bus.

"Did you hear him?! We're gonna move on! We're gonna win!"

Around school, the girls who had been involved with the stealing were angry and told Devin and the other girls that they had no chance of winning the Section V title if they were not on the team, but that just made Devin and the other girls more resolute.

"She caught fire after that," said Englert.

"They kept saying 'You're not going to be able to do anything this year' and they did," remembered Dineen. "She was our leader. She was the rock."

A week later, on June 5th, 2008, the Wayland-Cohocton Varsity Girls Track team won the league title by one point. They went undefeated in the regular season.

A week later, Devin ran a pivotal third leg of the 4x800 at the State Qualifiers Meet, starting only a few steps ahead and ending with a huge lead. The girl running the fourth leg, Abby Decker, took them even further ahead. The girls beat the school record by sixteen seconds. That same relay group won fourth place at the State Finals on June 15, 2008.

"I think it takes an extra something in a person to be successful in an event like that," said Alyssa Englert. "If you falter, your team falters."

Graduation finally came on June 29th. Devin is seen in her mother's picture albums wearing a yellow, black and white dress which is covered by her maroon cap and gown. She has an Army ribbon draped over her robes. Her hair is light blonde and her eyes are smiling. On her feet, she wears bright neon green and pink shoes that she picked out days before because, like so many of her fellow graduates, she wanted to stand out.

"She wanted to make a mark on the world," Dineen said once in an interview. "She wanted to make a difference."

Devin had grown into a mature student and an incredible athlete, and perhaps more importantly, into a young woman confident enough to desire experiences that would challenge her in new ways. She was not done growing. She was ready to extend her physical training and test her mental toughness, and soon she would find out that she was stronger than she knew.

Part 2: Ambition

"…if I stay here
And fight about Troy, I'll never return to my home,
But men will remember my glory forever. On the other hand,
If I go back to the precious land of my fathers,
No glory at all will be mine, but life, long life,
Will be, and no early death shall ever come on me."
--Homer, *The Iliad*, Book IX

Chapter 6: Becoming a Soldier

I, _____, do solemnly swear (or affirm) that I will support and defend the Constitution of the United States against all enemies, foreign and domestic; that I will bear true faith and allegiance to the same; and that I will obey the orders of the President of the United States and the orders of the officers appointed over me, according to regulations and the Uniform Code of Military Justice. So help me God."
    -Oath of the US Army

Devin began basic training on August 21, 2008 at Fort Leonard Wood, Missouri. When she arrived at "Fort Lost-in-the-Woods," she stepped off the bus and was greeted by screaming drill sergeants who told her and the rest of the maggots to line up. After being offered some loud words of encouragement, Devin began filling out the paperwork necessary for processing.

The drill sergeants separated the women and men and the four women transferred to a new company. The sergeants sorted them into platoons and the women were put together from that first day onward. They had their bunks together in a large bunkhouse, where hundreds of bunk beds stood in rows about two feet away from each other, with one wall locker for each.

With no time for socializing, the women, like the men, did what they were told and tried not to make mistakes that would affect the others. Men and women participated in the drills and training together. Waking up early, they learned the standard physical training regimen that they would continue for the whole of basic combat training (BCT). They learned marching and counting off. They memorized the ranks. They were punished and pushed to do more. They were tired, but had to force themselves to pay attention to classes on how to operate the Humvee, how to change a tire, and how to use the equipment inside. Training to drive a Humvee also meant being able to maneuver it in tight places, to drive over logs and mounds of dirt, and through deep pools of water without stalling out.

This continued for eight weeks, without a break.

Other aspects of the training included team development courses, such as getting a whole group across a series of obstacles using only a few planks. They had to learn basic medical training, such as the nerve-wracking task of putting an IV in without making the commanding officer bleed too much. They learned the all-too-necessary skills of tying tourniquets and carrying someone on a litter.

Soldiers entered gas chambers and removed their masks, tried not to breathe and but failed. Stumbling and coughing on the way out, holding masks above their heads with one hand, they held the shoulder of the soldier in front, eyes closed on the way out.

"Keep your hand on your battle buddy!" the sergeants yelled.

Then they reached fresh air, walking in a line, flapping arms like fools, trying not to pass out or puke.

The days were long; the breaks were short.

At one point, they completed a bayonet assault course. In the heat and dressed in full fatigues, Devin and her new brothers and sisters ran past signs that read "Thrust!" as the drill sergeant yelled "Run! You're being chased by al-Qaeda." Then stabbing colored vehicle tires, they yelled "Kill!"

Later, the recruits went head to head in a bayonet fight simulation. They had duels with the pugil stick, which looks like a broomstick with pads at both ends. Each recruit wears a helmet and all of the others sit around them in a circle. The only goal is to knock the other person down.

Another challenge was called "The Warrior Tower," which taught repelling skills. Physical endurance and confidence courses, what we civilians usually think of when we think of Basic Training, included obstacles like cargo nets, crawling through long drainage conduits, crawling through mud, jumping over walls, crossing a rope bridge, and commando crawling a single rope. These are intended to develop confidence and promote teamwork and problem solving skills.

Later, Advanced Individual Training (AIT) for Devin meant Military Police (MP) training, which included many training topics, like Advanced Communications and Advanced Map Reading skills, carbine and rifle training, vehicle and weapons checks, driving courses, M9 pistol qualification, law enforcement operations, detainee operations, active shooter response, and battlefield forensics. Much of this was done in an Army training complex that includes "a variety of building styles such [as] family housing, the theater, barracks, a snack bar and a mock MP station."[33]

In the midst of the intensity of Basic Training and AIT, Devin got to know the people around her everyday very well. Some of them she liked, and some of them she did not. She was able to hold her own, but she did not appreciate how some of the women were treated.

The first time that Jessica Jeffords ever noticed Devin was in formation, on the drill floor. They were at the new barracks at Fort Wood, waiting for the sergeants to talk. Sweating in their green Army Combat Uniforms (ACUs) with two-quart canteens slung over their shoulders, they stood by at parade rest. They were allowed to talk in parade rest, so for the females in the unit, they knew that meant taunting. Jeffords was lined up next to Devin, in the middle of three lines.

There was a particular young man who liked to make crude jokes. His comments inevitably led to sexual innuendos and blatant harassment of women, Jeffords especially. She always seemed to be lined up near him, and had to listen to his taunts. It was wearing her down a bit, and she was dreading every stop because she knew it would continue. She had been on edge because the harassment never seemed to end. It was at that moment of exhausted frustration that Jeffords heard a voice. It was Devin. She was suddenly berating the very large man who had been harassing Jeffords all day. Devin kept her right foot still, so she would not leave parade rest, but leaned over to him and screamed threats and obscenities in his face.

"Leave her alone!"

If nothing else, this embarrassed the man and got the attention of the officers, halting the harassment temporarily. However, this outburst of indignant rage showed the men in their platoon that there were women among them with grit. For Devin, it set her apart as one who was not to be toyed with. She was a soldier, and she held them to that standard.

This girl is crazy, thought Jeffords with a smirk. But a friendship was forged.

"You're around a bunch of guys who think they can say whatever they want," said David Saxton, later, about women in the military. "So they're going to."

For the most part, Devin was left alone. Growing up with her brother Damien strengthened her and meant that she was not intimidated by men. Other soldiers gave her respect for her athleticism and toughness.

"I think it's really hard to act that way around someone who is just fundamentally good like she was," reflected Saxton. "I think when guys get bested in a lot of things, and on paper I think she looked like a stellar soldier, they'd be like *damn*. What you look like on paper, to the big army, is all that matters. Down at our level, companies, battalions, brigades, it's you as a person as well, I think. She didn't take shit. You're not going to pursue it for that long if you get shut down."

In addition to having the guts to stand up for herself and the other females, Devin was one of three women in basic training to have already passed the Army Physical Fitness Test. All of her years of soccer and track helped her in that.

"She was a PT stud," said Jeffords.

"She got perfect scores in her PT things and she'd get awards for it, only they stopped giving them to her because she was getting them all of the time," remembered Aunt Danette.

That fall passed quickly. In November, Barack Obama was elected President of the United States. His policy was to end the war in Iraq and focus on Afghanistan, where he would send an additional 10,000 troops to supplement the 33,000 that were already there. He argued that the 150,000 troops in Iraq needed to be shifted to Afghanistan.[34]

Too busy to keep in close contact with everyone back home, Devin mostly lost touch. She missed the Spud Jug game and Fall Foliage weekend for the first time in years. Like many young adults leaving home to start a life of her own, she lost friendships with some and gained friendships with others.

"Yeah, it just happens with a lot of friends, especially in this area," said Emily May, highlighting another effect of the lack of economic opportunity in Western New York. "She went off somewhere, I went off somewhere, and my best friend Cait went off somewhere. It's common and it's hard to keep in touch and I feel bad, but that's what happens."

Before Christmas time, she had a two-week break for "Hometown Recruiting." She naturally went to the school during the day with her mom. She visited with her old teachers and spoke with people who wanted to know more about the military. She was reunited with old friends like Mikayla Sick.

"I would go every study hall to the computer lab," said Sick. "Devin and I would sit under the desk and watch *Forrest Gump*."

Devin's appearance had changed some. She had many tattoos on her arm, almost a whole sleeve finished.

Her great-uncle, Judge Snyder remembered seeing her at the time.

"I'm thinking that in time I don't think she would have stuck it out with the military," he said. "My impression at that time was she would have gotten all she could out of the military and then come home. I think she was destined for bigger and better things. It wouldn't have surprised me if she would have gone into the FBI."

Ironically, that impression of her, that she could do more than the military, came from the kind of growth and maturation that she experienced as a direct result of being in the military.

"When she was in the military, she thrived," remembered her uncle Greg McInnis. "She probably did better in the service than she would have done in college."

McInnis noticed that she had become somewhat more calm and confident.

"[She was] more level, more adult," he said. "She could come up here and seek advice and help with finances. That's when I saw her more than anything. She became an adult."

On January 15, 2009, about six months after high school graduation, Devin graduated from basic training. Her family traveled to see the ceremony. She was awarded a certificate for exceptional achievement.

On January 20, 2009, Barack Obama was inaugurated in Washington, DC.

Chapter 7: Alaska

Seven young women went from basic at Fort Leonard Wood to Fort Richardson, near Anchorage, Alaska in February of 2009. There, Devin Snyder joined the 164th MP Company, called the Arctic Enforcers. She and Jessica Jeffords were both assigned to the Third Platoon of the Fourteenth MP Brigade. They were taken to barracks and were able to choose a roommate, so they chose each other. They were the only two women were in the third platoon at Fort Richardson.

Sergeant Scott Enlow had already been in Alaska for a while. A few years earlier he had deployed to Iraq and served for seven months, but then was injured and was medically evacuated.

"Pulled myself together and went to Afghanistan with 164," he said. "I heard it was the best kept secret in the army. Got there in the state of Alaska and met a whole new batch of wonderful people."

"It's kind of cheesy but there's a quote that a lot of people don't understand why, but all it really is about is the man and woman next to you. That's all it's really about."

Enlow was given the opportunity to become a squad leader when his predecessor was fired. He had a rapport with the first sergeant and was appointed as one of the squad leaders of the Third Platoon.

"I had my squad and there were two senior squad leaders, meaning they outranked me. So I was the junior guy."

It was winter. Many of the soldiers' duties were inside. They spent most of their time in the motor pool. More like a warehouse, it hosted over 200 vehicles all lined up with military precision, or "dress-right-dress."

The MPs trained on gun ranges, with grenades, 249s and M4s. They learned to clean the guns, and to run the appropriate checks on them that they would need to do each day before operations.

"It was our first week up there," remembered Jessica, amused. "She was so small, and the guns were so big. She couldn't hit shit."

Once when their platoon went snowshoeing, Devin, who was always at the front of any run, temporarily felt what it was like to come in last. She was a bit pigeon-toed and kept stepping on her own snowshoe. Jessica laughed as Devin clumsily tried again and again, only to fall in the snow. They were wearing their heavy rucksacks and Jessica had to help her up out of the snow. Needless to say, they were late returning from morning PT.

"I made fun of her a lot for that," said Jessica.

In March, an earthquake shook the Pacific Ocean, sending a tsunami that would devastate Japan. About a week later, warnings came that Mount Redoubt, a nearby active volcano, might erupt. Devin and Jessica didn't have a real kitchen in their barracks, only a fridge, but they followed the recommendations and stocked up on drinking water and food.

The next morning, Jessica and Devin were on a run when a friend in a patrol car pulled them over.

"Hey, you guys need to get inside," he told them. "No one is supposed to be outside. A volcano just erupted."

Mt. Redoubt had erupted several times in the night, sending ash north of Fort Richardson. Cable news sources reported that the ash was sometimes "used as an industrial abrasive" because it can "injure skin, eyes and breathing passages."[35] Because of this threat, and the possibility of another eruption, the airport and the base shut down, and only essential staff was required to report. Jessica and Devin were told not to open the windows, go outside, start the car, or go to work. They were to stay inside.

After a while, it didn't seem to them like anything was abnormal, so Jessica and Devin snuck outside, out a back door where no one would see them, to have a cigarette. They were outside smoking and talking for a bit, looking around at the eerily quiet base, noticing not a single patrol car, not a single other soul.

"All of a sudden, I'm smoking and she's like 'stop ashing your cigarette on me' and I'm not. So she looks and there's ash on her shoulder on her jacket and it's like burning through the jacket…kind of melts into the jacket… She was wearing a North Face that she loved. We start seeing ash fall everywhere."

The sky was dark and gray "snowflakes" were falling. They decided to go inside.

At around the same time, the Obama Administration announced a change in the Afghanistan strategy. President Obama said in a speech:

"Multiple intelligence estimates have warned that Al Qaeda is actively planning attacks on the United States homeland from its safe haven in Pakistan. And if the Afghan government falls to the Taliban or allows Al Qaeda to go unchallenged, that country will again be a base for terrorists who want to kill as many of our people as they possibly can."

In order to prevent that, Obama proclaimed, "...we will shift the emphasis of our mission to training and increasing the size of Afghan security forces so that they can eventually take the lead in securing their country. That's how we will prepare Afghans to take responsibility for their security and how we will, ultimately, be able to bring our own troops home. For three years, our commanders have been clear about the resources they need for training. And those resources have been denied because of the war in Iraq. Now, that will change...The additional troops that we deployed have already increased our training capacity. And later this spring, we will deploy approximately 4,000 U.S. troops to train Afghan security forces."[36]

After a transition period in which government competency was built and new military forces were trained, the US would transfer power fully to Afghan security forces. The new policy could be boiled down to four words: Clear, Hold, Build, Transfer.

It was around that time that Devin bought a blue four-wheeler. She was very proud but customized it and painted it pink. She and Jessica starting hanging out with civilian friends who also had ATVs. They'd borrow one from a friend, and ride up into the nature preserve. It was a location high in the mountains, with long distance views and wildlife. They found a spot next to a river where there was no cell service. Devin often went there to find peace.

They did many of the things that other young adults did. There were house parties, movies, shopping, and hockey games.

That summer the two young women bummed a ride on a coast guard flight arranged by Jessica's uncle to Kodiak Island. There they ate fresh caught halibut deep fried in pancake batter, and later they tricked her uncle into seeing a "chick flick" at the local movie theatre.

On August 7th, on Devin's birthday, there was a fight on post, of all things. There were many people involved and many injuries. Jessica was hit with beer bottle while putting handcuffs on someone. After the commotion settled down, she took off her hat and saw blood everywhere, blacked out, and was taken to the hospital. When she came to, Jessica called Devin to tell her that she would not be coming out for her birthday that evening because of the injury. Devin canceled her plans and went to the hospital, spent the night there, and when they finally released Jessica, Devin drove her home. She took care of her friend.

That Christmas, Devin and Jessica did not go home. They stayed on base but then snuck off for the night to Alyeska Ski Resort with their civilian friends. They went four-wheeling and then snowboarding under the lights at night and had fun. The next morning, thinking that his squad might be feeling lonely, or perhaps trying to catch anyone who'd gone AWOL for the night, Sgt. Enlow recalled everyone to take them out for brunch. When Devin and Jessica got the message, they were already late. In a panic, they began packing, getting their story straight, and loading the car. Devin returned a rented board and put Jessica's on top of the car, but forgot to secure it, and it fell off somewhere along the highway as they hurried home. When they arrived, the entire squad had been waiting about an hour for them, but since it was Christmas, they were forgiven and they all went out to eat.

The next spring, in March, word came around that a special group was going to go to the Philippines to train the Philippine Army, and in turn, be trained by them. The group was to be selected from the whole company, so they had a contest to see who would go. Shooting, running, push-ups, sit-ups, and navigation were all aspects of the contest, and about six people from Devin's platoon were selected to go. There were about fourteen people total who took a civilian flight from Alaska to Seattle, then to Japan and the Philippines. Scott Enlow was one of the sergeants.

Jessica and Devin both won a seat. When they were packing and getting ready, they decided to buy a book and then they could switch after they finished.

"We just need to make sure we don't get the same book," said Devin.

"We won't get the same book," said Jessica.

But at some point on the trip, they noticed that they had done just that. It was *The Last Song* by Nicholas Sparks. They had one hardcover and one paperback.

The group reported to Fort Magsaysay, the largest military base in the Philippines, where large groups of Guam's National Guard and American Marines stationed in Japan were sent for a similar training. Philippine Army soldiers were also stationed on the base.

"Snyder and I, because we were females, we had to go to the female bay," said Jessica. "It was on the Marines side and we had to walk by all the Marines to get to the female area so we were being whistled at and hit on constantly while walking to our beds."

They had to leave one side of the base, go through a gate, cross the road, enter another gate, and walk to the very back of the other side to their barracks. One day, a large forest fire was burning nearby and threatening the safety of the base.

They were at the bazaar at the time watching an artist hand carve figurines. They ate unhatched chicken egg, a delicacy of the Philippines, and Jessica taught Devin the words to "Hotel California," by The Eagles, when the karaoke version came on. They ate ice cream together and were happy.

The call came to them to return to base, so they took a taxi back quickly and saw fire trucks going toward base while other military personnel, including the Marines, abandoned the base, leaving Devin and Jessica far from their rooms and without a ride. They hiked through the large base and carried five bags and their weapons on their backs, with the help of a couple of the guys, to the secure location. They could smell the smoke but were not sure if they needed to evacuate.

Eventually, the fire was contained and they could go back, but the emergency made it clear that Devin and Jessica really needed to be closer to their group, so they were given new barracks assignments on the same side as the men in their group, with some of the Filipino women who worked in the kitchens and supply warehousing.

No longer subject to the taunts of a whole company of Marines, Devin and Jessica could focus on the purpose of the mission. They began jungle survival training not long after that. They stayed near a beautiful cove, in a beachside "hut" that had the luxury of running water and a toilet. Devin and Jessica were given the only bedroom, while the guys slept on the floor. It was payback for the long walk to the previous barracks.

Out in the jungle, they learned primitive survival skills such as fire-starting using rocks, leaves, and bamboo fibers. They learned how to use bamboo to boil water, how to catch fish with their hands (though Jessica admits that she and Devin cheated a bit and stabbed the fish), and how to build a survival shelter. They learned to open coconuts and drank the cool juice. They ate ants for protein, and her food bit Devin a little. The trainers showed them wild tobacco, which they peeled off and chewed green.

"It was crazy how much they had in their forest just right there," observed Jessica. "They knew exactly what it was and they showed us poisonous plants and plants you could eat as a salad and there's an herb sort of like aloe vera for sunburns."

In the evenings, Devin and the others would sing karaoke with the guys from the Philippine Army. They loved Jessica and Devin's bright eyes, were spellbound by the green and blue, and a few marriage proposals were offered.

They kept saying, "Mahal kita," a Togalog phrase meaning "I love you." Devin and Jessica, not knowing what the phrase meant, repeated it back. Traditionally, this signified the beginning of a courtship when they said it back. One of their platoon members, taking advantage of the situation, jokingly tried to sell them both into marriage. When he was offered a goat, he replied, "Okay! I would have taken three eggs."

The Philippine Army was ill equipped, Jessica recalls. Some people had helmets, some had vests, and some had guns, but few had all three. The American MPs taught the Philippine MPs how to do interviews, read body language, and detain suspects. They spent a whole day at the range, teaching them to shoot.

On another evening, Devin, Jessica, and a few others decided to go on a hike and climbed up a nearby mountain. On a trail next to a cliff, Devin thought she saw a snake. She was deathly afraid of snakes and jumped back, running into Jessica. It turned out to be a discarded snakeskin, but in her panic, she pushed Jessica, who fell down a hillside and badly twisted her ankle.

"They were all laughing and I was laughing at first and then I realized how much pain I was in," said Jessica.

She took off her boot and it was so swollen, she couldn't put the boot back on. So she put on multiple socks as a makeshift cast.

The next morning they went to a tree obstacle course. It was high in the air and there were no safety harnesses.

Jessica sat by. There was no hospital near them, and she had no crutches, so she had to tough it out for the rest of the training.

That included leading training for the Philippine Army on hand-to-hand combat. She and another soldier had attended Combative School at Fort Riley in Kansas, where soldiers learn to fight and even compete in a UFC-style ring. They were trainers for their platoon and conducted the same training for the Philippine Army.

"It was fun, but they didn't like it at all," said Jessica. She was kind of amused at that.

Later, since she needed to keep her foot up, Jessica picked up the novel she had brought. Devin went out to play basketball with some of the guys and when she returned, Devin found Jessica crying. Worried for her friend, Devin asked if she was okay, but Jessica said it was fine. It was just the book. Devin laughed, and then made fun of her for a few days.

Toward the end of the trip, a higher-ranking officer with the Philippine Army came out to the cove where they were staying to bring the group an Asian specialty sometimes called "snake wine." The man brought cobras, but in the process, was bitten by one and had to rush away to get anti-venom. His assistant took over and cut off the heads, showing them where the venom glands were, and then poured pure grain alcohol into the snake and then drained it out, mixing his libations, and poured out shots for everyone.

Jessica, still in pain from the injury, decided to sit this one out.

"I was a little too grumpy to do it and thought it was disgusting," she said.

Devin, still eager to experience all that she could, downed a shot in one gulp. It is believed that the blood of the snake is invigorating for warriors and healing for the sick. Other types of snake wine are sold to tourists all throughout Asia. Usually, a snake is dropped into a bottle and then it is filled with rice wine or alcohol and allowed to sit for a few months to make the tincture. Devin and the others had theirs fresh.

Afterward, they had grilled cobra with rice for dinner as the sun went down. That night they had a going away party with the Philippine Army and Devin and Jessica snuck a few beers. They ate a feast and sang karaoke late into the night.

In the middle of the night, it was time to depart, and they gathered their gear and rode, most of them passed out, to the airport. They were sitting outside on the ground and waiting, and other people were there waiting for planes.

Devin was waiting and reading the book that had so captivated Jessica.

"She finally finished the book and she was bawling her eyes out," said Jessica.

With everyone there to see, the others made fun of her for a while to pass the time.

Back in Alaska, Jessica and Devin truly enjoyed the long days of summer.

"It was kind of nice. We were so young that we didn't care about anything anyway."

Devin was continually great at PT. She always was good at boards. She was soldier of the month more than once and she had perfect 300 on the physical fitness test. This helped her to get noticed and she was promoted twice, from Private to Private First Class, and then to Specialist.

She and Jessica were inseparable.

"We fought when someone left without the other," said Jeffords.

One time while Jessica was away for training, Devin borrowed Jessica's car and got a flat tire but parked it. Jessica got back two months later to find a car with a flat tire. To get back at her, she stole her ID. Devin was locked out and had to climb in through a window.

About this time, Devin began seeing Sgt. Eric Hubbard. She sought him out and he gave her advice about how to succeed in the Army and how to get promoted and the friendship developed from there. She liked his commitment and professionalism, and appreciated his Kentucky style and lifted pickup truck.

One day, Jessica and Devin were hanging out and Hubbard's roommate came up to them with some civilian wildlife workers. They had found a mother bear living in the mountainous area of the base with several small cubs. They had tranquilized and tagged them for relocation and brought them around to show people. Devin and Jessica were allowed to hold one of the cubs for a moment.

"They were super heavy," said Jessica.

Unfortunately for Devin and Eric, it was Army policy that soldiers were not to date soldiers of higher rank. Though the two had great affection for each other, their military careers were more important to them both and they called it off.

Devin and Jessica decided to start going on Army-paid recreational outings, called Single Soldier Retreats. They hiked a glacier, went to concerts, went on a fishing boat, went horseback riding, snowmobiling, and visited the SeaLife Center in Seward, AK. They were young and found things to do to feed their hunger for experience.

In April, some new troops came to Fort Richardson. One of them was Stacey Jordan, a young woman from Belmont, NY, a small town in Allegheny County not far from Cohocton, NY.

"There's nothing there," said Stacey, chuckling. "There's not much to do. It was either partying or getting in trouble somewhere."

She was working about twenty hours a week at a local nursing home after high school. Well aware of the foolishness of the dead end drug scene, she went into the military.

"I wasn't really the college type of person," said Stacey. "Me and my dad liked to shoot guns and get dirty and blow up things. I was a tomboy. I hated school."

Like many families on the border of northern Appalachia and the Rust Belt, there were few local opportunities. Her sister had dropped out of nursing school and her parents would already have to pay that debt. They couldn't take on any more, so they encouraged her to see the world through the Army instead.

"Go, travel," they said to her. "Go experience the world. Go do things you wouldn't be able to do if you were just a civilian." The Army was the only way for her to do those things.

So she did. Not only with the Army, but on her own. As she made new friends, she had greater opportunities to travel and visit people during leave.

"If I didn't join the army I don't even think I would have seen half the states that I've seen. Every six months when we had break, I would go home for a week and then I'd go travel."

In Alaska, there were only five or six other women in their company's barracks, so Devin and Stacey would inevitably get to know each other.

Stacey's first impression was that Devin was kind of intimidating.

"When new people come in you kind of bully them," she remembered about Fort Richardson, "When she had to yell or discipline soldiers, she would do it. She wasn't that nice girl that was like 'Hey, don't do it again.' She'd get up in their face and scream at them. When I first met them, her and Jessica, Devin was yelling at a soldier and I was new and scared and nervous."

To Stacey, Devin was clearly an excellent soldier of higher rank who had high standards. She was not afraid to tell people that they were not meeting those standards. In addition, she was also always with Jessica, and their relationship could seem like a barrier for Stacey to get to know either of them. Stacey, already a shy person, didn't really have the confidence to talk to her.

"The first couple months we didn't really talk because she was always with Jessica," remembered Stacey.

But Jessica was no longer going to deploy. Her injury in the Philippines was greater than she thought, and because she had not received any medical attention at the time, it made the injury worse. She had to have surgery and would heal, but would not be going to Afghanistan.

Eventually, in part because of their deployment orders, Devin and Stacey warmed up to each other and became friends.

"When we actually got to know each other we were like 'oh my god' we probably played soccer against each other," remembered Stacey. "We live forty minutes away from each other so we kind of clicked. We were roommates, we did everything together."

Stacey looked up to Devin at the time, who was their team leader and such a strong athlete and soldier.

"She walked it," said Stacey.

Devin developed a reputation for being a tough but fair team leader. She would not abuse her authority like some might, and lazily assign members of her team to do things she was assigned. She was part of the team, and would help when there was work to do.

"She wanted to make the Army better," said Stacey.

Stacey idolized Devin through that time. She tried to learn as much as she could from her and even offered a listening ear when Devin needed to vent her frustrations about the Army or personal matters.

After being together for so long, Jessica and Devin were now spending more and more time apart. Their relationship quirk of getting angry when one person went somewhere without the other still seemed to apply, even though they both must have known, logically, that deployment meant separation. They began to grow apart, though they still spent time together with their larger group of friends.

At the same time, Devin began to get closer to Stacey Jordan, who became almost like one of her track sisters. Or in this case, her deployment sister. They started doing most things together.

There was discord in the "Big Army" as well. In May, General David McKiernan was removed as top commander in Afghanistan and replaced with General Stanley McChrystal.[37] He soon publicly asked for more troops in Afghanistan. If the strategy of General Petraeus and President Obama was to work, if they were going to build a secure Afghanistan, then they would need more troops.

But life went on. People enjoyed Devin for who she was.

"She was a goof and clumsy," said Stacey. "Sergeant Vetterkind would say she would trip over air. We'd be walking to the chow hall or something and she would trip out of nowhere."

Jessica's surgery came and her mom came to help out. Devin had to leave for deployment training. She left Jessica a card that read:

Jeffords,

You're my best friend and you better know I will always be there for you just like I know you'll always be there for me. I hope your surgery went good... when I get back we can go around acting all crazy like usual—even with you in your boot, haha.

Love you,
Snyder

Chapter 8: Reversal

Stacey Jordan left with Devin and others to California for a month of deployment training. They were supposed to deploy in November. The training consisted of hours of role-playing, with Stacey and Devin often playing the role of the Afghanis.

Stories of Devin's adventures came home to family and friends through Dineen.

"She just was adventurous and she basically was just taking on the world full force," said Danette McInnis, remembering that time. "Taking in every moment."

Upon their return to Alaska, the routine returned. Being a woman in the military was a challenge, even for a good soldier. If not the object of direct harassment, then certainly Devin and the other women were at least the butt of many jokes.

"The Army frowned upon them really coming out and saying females were weaker," said Stacey, "but we get treated different."

A group of women might get orders to move something heavy, knowing it would be impossible for them to do it. The higher-ranking soldiers would laugh. Or during combatives, Stacey would be matched up with a 200-pound man. She would have to try to take him down, and the surrounding soldiers would laugh.

"They just watched us struggle," she said.

Some of that might be just immature men setting them up to fail, some of it might be training to prepare our female soldiers for war and the possibility that they might encounter a dominant enemy.

"I mean our platoon was so close it was more like just joking around," said Stacey, but women in general were still regarded as the weaker sex.

"Devin was one of the top kids in the company. She proved that wrong."

Stacey never felt unsafe, but she knew where she stood.

"They were like brothers," said Stacey.

One time someone did cross the line: Devin's First Sergeant. During a week in the field, the soldiers were conducting training exercises and combat drills. At one point, Devin and Stacey were assigned to watch the weapons tent while the others ate.

"Our first sergeant came in and we were talking for a little bit. She was down on the one end of the tent and he was in the middle of us." He got close to Devin and she tried going around him, but he was blocking the way. Finally, "he grabbed Devin," said Stacey, "and laid her on the ground and straddled her."

"Devin freaked out. She flipped," said Stacey.

"Get off!" Stacey yelled. But then she became timid. *He's our first sergeant, our company commander,* she thought. "Why are you doing this?!"

"So we went off and told Sgt. Enlow," said Stacey. "We got interviewed. That time it was kind of scary and stuff. He actually got relieved for doing that."

Afterward, they were completely in shock. Stacey felt betrayed since he was their First Sergeant.

"We felt weird about it. It was weird. But that happened. I don't even know if she told a lot of people about that. I'm glad he got in trouble."

"I mean, it does happen. You probably have one or two. Like, two in every company that will at least try. For the most part our platoon was really close and they were all pissed off and wanted to punch him. They had our backs. Overall, they did have our backs. Even if we had a bad day and were crying, they would be right there."

When she got back to base, Devin tried to make Jessica some bacon and eggs for breakfast, but burned it badly and set fire alarm off. Fire trucks came soon after.

In August, nearly their entire platoon decided to go the Alaska State Fair. It was about an hour drive from base. Devin and Stacey both dressed in civilian clothes and joined the group.

"We had our hair down, in curls. We looked like girls," said Jordan.

They were walking around the tents and saw a palm reader. Devin paid the $35 and the woman inside began reading her palm. Stacey sat nearby.

"She didn't know anything about us except our first names," said Jordan.

The woman told Devin that she saw that she was in a relationship, but that it was kind of rocky and that the couple would need to work at it, if it was to get better.

Then she moved on to other lines in her palm.

"I see an ocean. Overseas."

"I see an ocean but you're not going over," continued the palm reader. "Wherever your coworkers are going, you're not."

"I see you're going to go far in your career."

Everyone else would be going, but not her. She would be staying back to work on things here, she told Devin.

Then it was Stacey Jordan's turn. The palm reader went through the usual routine, but when she came to the subject of the future, she told Stacey that, unlike Devin, she would be going across an ocean.

On the way back to base, Devin was still thinking about the palm reader. She questioned why her future was predicted as it was. She wondered why the fortune-teller would say such a thing. It seemed idiotic. The woman must have misread her hand.

"Why wouldn't I go over? There's nothing wrong with me," she said. It didn't make any sense. "We're leaving in a few months. How does she know that?"

Around that time, Damien finished basic training and went to Advanced Individual Training for 16 weeks at Fort Lee, Virginia. Then Ft. Carson, Colorado. Their relationship had grown from when they were children, bickering and teasing. Damien and Devin would talk once or twice a week. He would call her if he needed help.

"She knew all the answers," he said. "She was a board baby."

In November, Devin and Stacey's deployment was delayed and the Alaska winter was fully upon them. NATO committed to transferring security responsibilities to a force of 100,000 Afghans by 2014, called the "NATO-Afghanistan Enduring Partnership." They would need people to train and equip that security force. The US would honor that commitment by spending over $6 billion in foreign aid to Afghanistan between 2011 and 2014. About $4 billion of that went to the war during 2011, when Devin, Stacey, and their platoon were set to deploy.[38]

One day, a group of soldiers went outside to clear the snow off of the trucks. Devin and the others were dressed in full winter gear, complete with heavy boots, coats, and winter gloves. Everyone was fine and did their jobs, but after a short time, Devin took off her gloves and showed Stacey her hands. She didn't admit to being cold, but her entire hands were purplish, almost clear. The medic for her platoon made her go to the doctor to get tested.

The result was the only blemish on her record: "Not allowed to be outside in temperatures under 50."

She was diagnosed with Raynaud's Disease, which according to the Mayo Clinic, "is a condition that causes some areas of your body — such as your fingers, toes, the tip of your nose and your ears — to feel numb and cool in response to cold temperatures or stress. In Raynaud's disease, smaller arteries that supply blood to your skin narrow, limiting blood circulation to affected areas." It is not a seriously debilitating disease, but it can cause numbness in the fingers and toes.

"For a while, when we were working outside, she had to stay inside to do work," said Stacey.

Of course this was a problem. Afghanistan is a mountainous country, with cold winters at high elevations. It could affect her performance as a soldier. If so, it could endanger the group.

"They told her that they didn't want her to deploy because you never quite knew what could happen. If we were out on some mission or something, and we didn't have any access to any buildings, or if it got cold, they didn't want that to be a problem while we were out there."

"This isn't fair. This is what I joined to do," said Devin, crying later as she came into Stacey's room. "I would hate it if you guys went over and I wasn't there with you."

"She was so disappointed that she wasn't allowed to go," remembered Stacey. "She didn't want to be a shammer." A *shammer* is Army slang for an indifferent slacker. "I think she would have had a lot of guilt."

"She was not supposed to go," said Jessica, reflecting on it later.

Devin called her mother one day that November, crying.

"So finally they even had their unit picture done of those who were deploying and she wasn't able to be in that photo because she was not," remembered Dineen, "and that upset her more than anything. Sent her right over the edge."

If she was kept back, or worse, put on disability, it would be akin to telling her that she was handicapped. She would not be able to live with that. A medical discharge might as well have been a dishonorable one.

So, she decided to fight it.

"When the doctors told her that she wasn't supposed to go, she was telling all of her leadership that she was going whether they let her or not," said Jessica. "She didn't care what she had to do to get on that plane and go."

So, she was represented by one of the members of the leadership before the division commander, who was in charge of her commander.

"She had to explain why they were going to violate the doctor's order and why she wanted to go," said Stacey.

In this matter, Devin didn't really ask the leadership for permission, she just told them what she was going to do. Because she had been on the boards and was well-regarded, they heard her out.

"Devin spoke her mind and when she wanted something done, she was going to do it," said Stacey. "She wouldn't stop."

It is unclear if anything was resolved at the end of that meeting. The issue was dropped because the holidays were coming and Devin went home for leave.

On December 1st, President Obama gave a speech at West Point, announcing a troop increase:

"As commander in chief, I have determined that it is in our vital national interest to send an additional 30,000 U.S. troops to Afghanistan. After 18 months, our troops will begin to come home. These are the resources that we need to seize the initiative, while building the Afghan capacity that can allow for a responsible transition of our forces out of Afghanistan."[39]

Only days later, Dineen got a call from her mother and stepfather. They were coming home from Rochester, making the familiar drive south along the interstate, after doing some shopping.

"We thought we would just drop off what we got you for Christmas because it's kind of big," said her mom, "and rather than wait until Christmas, it would just be easier to bring it to the house."

"You can wait," Dineen replied. "We can bring the truck or whatever."

"Oh, no, we just want to drop it off."

Dineen's stepfather brought in what looked like a used suitcase and put it on the floor.

"Oh, thanks?" said Dineen, trying to be nice.

"I know my reactions spoke volumes," she remembered. "All of a sudden Devin popped around the corner. I lost it. It was so cute. She got to spend two weeks with us at Christmas."

Dineen and Ed and their family learned more about the Raynaud's issue that Christmas. The Army doctors had tried prescribing blood pressure medication, but Devin started getting light-headed as a side effect. They tried adjusting the dosage, then other medications as well, but Raynaud's is incurable and difficult to manage.

During the holidays, Devin visited with friends and family. Danette and Greg heard that Devin was fighting to be able to deploy.

"We were thinking she was not going to go," said Greg.

Devin had been talking to them about other opportunities in the Army, if she was unable to convince the leadership. As a backup plan, she was interested in becoming a K9 dog handler.

She had resolved herself to finding an interesting life, even if she didn't deploy, but the disappointment she felt was always on her mind, in the background of the holiday festivities.

It was mostly a waiting game, until after the holiday season. So the Snyders simply enjoyed each other's company at home.

"That was our last Christmas," said Dineen.

Later, the topic came up again. Devin and Dineen were sitting in the living room and talking on the leather couch.

"They're not going without me," said Devin.

"You can't push it," said Dineen. "Maybe there's a reason this is happening. Maybe it's a warning."

"No. I have to go. This is what I signed up for," said Devin.

Dineen eventually had to let it go. It was Devin's life to live as she chose. Her mind was set. It was time to listen to Devin and support her choice, even if Dineen felt uneasy about that choice.

"She was excited," remembered Natasha. "At that time she still wasn't a hundred percent sure she was going to go or not. I told her specifically that she needed to listen to the doctors. But her mindset was that she was going to go and that's what she wanted to do. She didn't want to leave her unit."

They were nervous, but Natasha had deployed multiple times. In her eight years of service, she worked directing helicopters on aircraft carriers in the Persian Gulf. She earned her shellback certificate (for crossing the equator) in her tenure, and had been to ports in Costa Rica, Puerto Rico, Spain, Italy, Ireland, as well as locations in the Middle East, such as Israel, Dubai, and Bahrain.

The family understood, of course, that Natasha visiting places as a tourist while on liberty was not the same as Devin's job would be as an MP on the ground where she would be in direct contact with hostile forces.

"I had already been through a few deployments so I kind of knew what it was on my end of it," said Natasha. "I had no clue what she was about to go through."

For the most part, the Snyders enjoyed the Christmas season with family and friends as if it were any other year.

"We had fun and we laughed and we joked," said Natasha. "Mostly we were all trying to enjoy the time that we had with each other."

A point of pride for them, that was perhaps also a reassurance, was Shirley Saxton, Dineen's maternal grandfather, a veteran of WWII.

Devin went to visit him in an assisted care home when on leave during that time. Her elder relative had a hard time seeing Devin as a soldier.

"Back in my day, women weren't allowed in the Army. They could only be nurses," he said.

"Well, Grandpa, times have changed. They got me now," said Devin.

Mr. Saxton, who suffered from dementia, began reminiscing about his time in the Army.

"He just lit all up and started telling stories," remembered Dineen.

Christmas break ended and Devin continued to fight to deploy. Being a quitter or a failure was not acceptable for her.

She lived in that state of limbo for all of January of 2011. In February, for reasons even she didn't understand, Devin was given another short leave and decided to visit Colorado with Jessica, to meet her family and see something new. They worked at the family pizza place, made pizzas with all the sauces and toppings, went tubing with Jessica and her Dad and sister, and went to a college party. Jessica and Devin did as many things as they could in that short time.

When they returned to Alaska, Devin found out she would not deploy. Secretly, Jessica was thankful.

But it would not do for Devin. She went right up her chain of command and protested the decision. It was the moment when her greatest and most admirable trait, her determination, became her tragic flaw, the time in her life when she may have pushed too hard against the Fates. Relatives and friends think about that time and, even though there were many factors involved in her death, some wonder, "What if she hadn't?"

Finally, the Army ended up signing off.

"They [the command] said that she would be fine and they would take care of her," recalled Dineen. "They had equipment there in case, and they would mostly be in vehicles… Can't guarantee she'll be fine totally, but medically with the Raynaud's, they did say she would be fine with that."

"And all of a sudden Dineen says she's back on schedule," recalled Aunt Danette.

This reversal made Devin very happy. She would be going on a great journey, not staying behind. It may have been a relief to her as well. Foremost, it was a narrow avoidance of what was perhaps her greatest fear: that she would let her platoon down. But an additional relief may have been that she was not denied the outlet for her high energy and high hopes, nor an outlet for her years of military training.

"I think in her heart of hearts she felt like she was letting people down by not being able to go," said Dineen.

When Devin was given her deployment orders, word spread around the school. Coach Julie Martin heard from Dineen, but didn't picture Devin being in a combat zone.

"Even though I knew what her role in the military was, I didn't really think that she would be in danger."

"I cried when she called," said Natasha. "I honestly did not want her to go."

They spoke on the phone.

"Are you 100% positive?" asked Natasha.

"Yes," said Devin. "Everything is going to be fine."

Natasha's voice broke up again into tears.

"This is what I need to do. I need to go with my unit."

"Okay. We'll Skype. We'll email. Call me when you can."

Jessica, who would remain on rear deployment (rear D), had a 24-hour shift every other day. Her schedule was essentially to sleep one day and work the next.

Those who were deployed were getting excited. A few of them decided to blow off some steam in a friend's Jeep.

"The weekend before we deployed, Me, Devin, Rivera and Oslund went mudding," said Stacey.

Another friend of theirs brought his $500 truck. He didn't really care about it and kept taking on huge bumps at high speeds. Finally, the truck just stopped and wouldn't start. They knew they were deploying soon, and a few of the guys decided to set it on fire. Devin and Stacey sat in the car.

"We got in trouble. Well, we didn't get in real trouble," remembered Stacey. "We had to do baggage detail the next day for the plane. We could have gotten in a lot of trouble."

Back home, friends sent her messages through Facebook, wishing her well.

One was Tyler Austin, her childhood friend. They made plans to meet up when she returned from deployment the following July. Devin's parents speculate that there was something more than friendship between them.

"I think that they always should have been together," said Dineen. "If he had a problem he went to Devin, if Devin had a problem she went to Tyler. I think that Devin wanted to see where it would go and that's how she kind of left it."

"He should have been my son-in-law," said Ed. "I told him that."

"I talked to her the day before she deployed," said Natasha. "I asked if she was nervous and she said no, she was excited. We didn't talk for very long; I just told her to make sure you email me, keep me updated, I love you, I'll talk to you soon. That was about it."

A while before Devin had to leave for deployment, Jessica called to tell her that she was going to go to sleep for a few hours. She asked Devin to call her and wake her up before she left so she could come to say goodbye. For whatever reason, perhaps annoyed that Jessica wasn't there to see her off, Devin didn't call her.

Jessica woke up later in a panic and called Devin right away to ask her why.

Devin didn't seem to have a good answer.

"I don't say goodbye," she told Jessica. "It's not goodbye."

Jessica was mad and hurt. She had just wanted to see her one more time. They ended the phone call with some uneasiness between them. The tension remained after they hung up. They never directly spoke again.

But Jessica would be on Devin's mind when she deployed, as Jessica hid a scrapbook of photos of their friendship in her pack before she left. She would look through it fondly in Afghanistan.

Devin thought that she would see them all in July when she came home on leave, and they would go from there. They would have time to catch up later.

Devin Snyder as a young girl.

Devin Snyder at the Quarter Mile Kid's Run when she was 5.

Devin Snyder playing soccer.

Devin Snyder in high school.

Devin Snyder and one of her "track sisters," Alyssa Englert

Devin Snyder on a trip to Florida with her track team.

Dineen, Devin, and Ed Snyder at Devin's graduation from AIT.

Devin Snyder with her great-grandfather, Shirley Saxton, and great-grandmother, Gloria Saxton.

Devin and Dineen Snyder

Ed and Devin Snyder

Devin Snyder at home on Christmas

Devin Snyder and Jessica Jeffords during training in California

Jessica Jeffords and Devin Snyder at Jeffords' family pizza shop in Colorado

Devin Snyder in Afghanistan

Stacey Jordan and Devin Snyder in Afghanistan

Above and Below: The Forward Operating Base at Mihtarlam, Afghanistan

Devin Snyder in Mihtarlam, Afghanistan

Above and Below: School children, teachers, and members of the community in Cohocton, NY, awaiting the motorcade.

Preparations are made for the memorial service at the Cohocton Sports Complex.

A caisson carries Devin Snyder's remains to the memorial service. Her family walks behind.

Cohocton community members watch from above and mourn with the family.

Veterans stand by as color guard for the funeral procession.

Mourners of all ages gather near the highway to show their support.

A large boulder on the side of the highway painted by friends of Devin Snyder.

Boots and ID tags of the fallen.

Chapter 9: Deployment

Across the world from Cohocton, in the high mountains of Afghanistan, the snowy mountain peaks act as the minarets for humble villages made of mud brick and stone. The call to prayer echoes high above these settlements and the wide valleys below. Each small valley formed from mountain creeks is a tributary to only a handful of great river systems, most of which flow west toward Iran, having their origins in the Hindu Kush Mountains in the north, east and center of the country. Kabul and Jalalabad are deep in those northern regions and the mountain-born rivers flow down sometimes narrow, sometimes wide valleys. It is easy to imagine the first people to follow the rivers upstream into the mountains. They might have found their way blocked by high mountain peaks and snow, and thus began looking for an easier way.

Eventually, they found the one river in the area that flows east, the Darya-ye Kabul (Persian for "Kabul River"). It is a tributary of the Indus River system in Pakistan, crossing the border north of the Khyber Pass into Pakistan, near Peshawar. Over 400 miles long, the Kabul River provides a source of water for irrigation in the land through which it passes. It feeds one of the greatest river civilizations in human history, the Indus Valley Civilization.

The Kabul River has been an important access path for travelers since the first human explorers walked in its valley. It was the route that Alexander the Great took on his way to India. He knew it as the Kophes River. It later became part of the Silk Road. Today, the Kabul River valley hosts a highway that follows the river and the old Silk Road. Traveling east, one can drive from Kabul to Jalalabad, then through the Khyber Pass, to Peshawar, Pakistan in about four hours.

Continuing onward, along what is known as the Grand Trunk Road, which goes from Kabul and Peshawar, through Delhi, all the way to Calcutta, one arrives on the eastern side of India, with access to China. This makes the Kabul River Valley and the Khyber Pass the gateway to the Far East for Afghanistan.

This has been the case for perhaps thousands of years. In 1921, National Geographic published an article entitled "Everyday Life in Afghanistan," which describes the trade route as follows:

The trade of Afghanistan is moved entirely by caravans... through the famous Khyber Pass, the great gateway from India... This pass is open every week, on Tuesdays and Fridays, except in very hot weather, when it is available to trade only on Fridays. A most rigid scrutiny is exercised by the Amir's agents on all who come and go. As soon as caravans from India enter the country, their Indian leaders are turned back and heavily armed Afghan guides take their places... In the morning the Khyber Pass is open for caravans coming into Afghanistan, and in the afternoon for those routed in the opposite direction. The pass is absolutely closed between sundown and sun-up... Camels leaving the country are usually loaded with wool, skins, dried fruits and vegetables, assorted gums, and spices. Thousands of horses are also driven along for sale in India as cavalry and polo mounts.[40]

Since the Khyber Pass is part of the ancient Silk Road, and one of the oldest mountain-passes in the world, the long and winding road down the narrow valley of the pass has become a strategic military site. During Operation Enduring Freedom, US and NATO supplies from Pakistan came through the castle-like Khyber Pass Gate into Afghanistan. Unfortunately, it is also the route through which insurgents were, and are, smuggling arms and explosives from Pakistan.

One thing is certain: It is not an easy place to control.

Kabul and the Kabul River, for example, have been inhospitable places to Westerners since Alexander, who conquered and set up permanent forts and settlements in much of the western part of the country, but found that the tribes in the higher elevations nearer the Hindu Kush Mountains, according to Plutarch, were as difficult to subdue as the hydra.[41]

For the British Empire, it was no easy territory either. Kipling even wrote a poem called "Ford o' Kabul River," in which several of his fellow troops drowned while attempting to cross the Kabul River in the dark. In the last stanza, he warns:

Turn your 'orse from Kabul town
Blow the trumpet, draw the sword
'Im an' 'arf my troop is down,
Down an' drownded by the ford.

In the Anglo-Afghan Wars, the British invaded three different times. The first two times, they destroyed much of Kabul and deposed the current kings, but afterward were angered when the successive kings became close to Iran and Russia. The Muhammadzai Dynasty simply wanted the British and the Viceroy of India to stay out of their internal affairs, and this became the arrangement in 1878 when Britain again invaded and made Afghanistan a British protectorate, in charge of its foreign affairs. After failing during the Third Anglo-Afghan War, when Afghanistan declared independence, the British retreated to India and eventually acknowledged the sovereign Afghan state in 1921.[42]

It is enough to wonder why so many empires have even bothered to go into Afghanistan. The reasons are many, but the primary is that the mountains conceal enemy threats. Pro-Russian forces supported their Empire by conducting raids into British Territory, especially India. The British responded in kind and Afghanistan became both caravan trail and battle ground.

But the mountains also hide ancient treasures.

About 250 miles to the north of Kabul, deep in the mountains of Badakhshan Province, are the mines of Sar-i-Sang, where for seven thousand years or more, human beings have mined the deep blue stone called lapis lazuli. The mining area itself is about 150 miles long and 25 miles wide, and rests in the narrow Kokcha Valley, a landscape that is both difficult to traverse and dangerous to settle. Mining groups can only operate 6 months out of the year, if at all, since winter takes over the rest of the year at that altitude (about 18,000 feet). Wolf and wild boar populate the region and summer temperatures are scorching hot.

The city of Ur, in ancient Sumer, present day Iraq, was probably the first Mesopotamian city to procure the stone and use it for carvings and jewelry. It was from these mines that jewels came for the devotees of Ishtar, ancient Babylonian goddess of love and war. Her association with the stone can be found in *The Epic of Gilgamesh*. In it, she wears fly-shaped beads of lapis on her necklace and even promises Gilgamesh a chariot made of lapis if he will become her lover.

It was from these mines that lapis lazuli was taken for the burial mask of King Tut.

It was from these mines that the stone was taken and ground into paint pigments for the Renaissance artists who wished to paint Mary, mother of Jesus, in her brilliant blue robes.[43]

Taliban factions have discovered immense wealth in the illegal mining of lapis lazuli, so much so that it has become a major sources of income.

But it is not just the brilliant blue stone that the most modern miners seek, recent geological surveys have confirmed an estimated "$1 trillion in untapped mineral deposits in Afghanistan."[44] These deposits include gold, iron, copper, lithium, and rare earth metals (REEs). The first three on the list are traditional valuable metals. Lithium, however, is used in batteries for most modern wireless devices as well as for electric cars and home energy storage.[45] The increase in the use of these batteries will undoubtedly create a significant increase in demand for lithium in the near future, but it is the last group, the rare earth metals that may be the most valuable deposit. Used in the civilian world for "cellphones, televisions, hybrid engines, computer components, batteries, lasers, fiber optics, and superconductors," REEs are also vital to military technologies, such as "tank navigations systems, missile guidance systems, fighter jet engines, missile defense components, satellites, and military grade communications gear."[46]

China has already had copper mining contracts in place for some time, but their state-owned Metallurgical Group Corporation has yet to develop the mines due to "poor security and a lack of transport infrastructure." Taliban groups, rebranded "The Islamic Emirate of Afghanistan" after American withdrawal, promised to "provide security" for the Chinese firm.[47]

For much of its history, and especially for the last one hundred years, Afghanistan has been conquered, occupied, or in the chaotic state just following conquest or occupation. Traders have sought treasures from along the Silk Road and at its ends for centuries. Empires have come and gone. Persians, Greeks, Mongols, Arabs, Brits, and Russians have all made their mark on the country as it is today. And, to the locals, the people whose ethnic groups have inhabited the region for hundreds of years, the United States is no different.

The country as a whole was established as a union of the Pashtun tribal majority in 1747, pulling together the regional power centers of Herat, Kandahar, and Kabul. This, in addition to the whole of the Indus Valley (present-day Pakistan), became the domain of Ahmad Shah Durrani through a campaign of conquest and unification.

The terrain is largely mountainous and the location of Kabul, which has served as the capital for many regimes, is in a large basin surrounded by high peaks. It is essentially a natural fortress and this feature of the land has led to isolationism throughout Afghanistan's history, which is why is it was considered to be a buffer state in the conflicts between the British and the Russian Empires. These same rocky highlands contribute both to the development of regional and tribal identities and the subsequent internal political conflict between tribes like the Tajiks and Uzbeks.

Some of that tribal rivalry has set Afghanistan back a hundred years or more and prevented its development into a modern state. Foreign states such as Britain and Russia have pitted ethnic groups against each other in their own chess game for regional dominance and many of those old suspicions and hatreds have persisted through the years. The Taliban preyed upon those regional splits and won the civil war. The condition of the country afterward under the Taliban, who cared more for religious and social policy than economic development and infrastructure improvement, deteriorated to such an extent that it was even difficult for the United States to find targets worthy of our retaliatory missile strikes after 9/11.[48]

But we did find some. American ground troops did eliminate al Qaeda and Taliban strongholds, where terrorist attacks on American civilians were being planned.

Despite our original intent to destroy such strongholds, it may be that the spoils of war, the treasure in the mountains for the United States, is Afghanistan's proximity to other valuable states in the region. Afghanistan shares a border with both Iran and Pakistan. This means that US ground troops would be able to deploy to those countries, if the occasion should arise. Iraq also is on the other side of Iran, which means that the two wars against terrorism that the

United States has been fighting were and are directed toward two countries surrounding Iran, an outspoken critic of the US and one of George W. Bush's "Axis of Evil" countries. As an added value, Afghanistan is on the opposite side of Pakistan from our ally and the country with the 2nd most English-speaking people in the world, India. Both of those states, not coincidentally, have nuclear arms.

From a regional perspective, Afghanistan is just across the Persian Gulf from the world's third largest oil producer and one of our strongest military allies, Saudi Arabia. It would be naïve to omit any discussion of oil simply because Afghanistan does not have any. Crude oil development, as well as other imperial aims, has guided policy in the Middle East for at least 100 years. A quick internet search will reveal companies such as the Iraq Petroleum Company, or the Kuwait Oil Company, or the Anglo-Iranian Oil Company (now British Petroleum, or BP).

It's not hard to imagine why these companies and their parent countries were eager to develop the oilfields. Consider for a moment how truly miraculous oil is, as a substance. It is the power of the sun in a liquefied and commodified form. It is valuable, like gold, and powerful, like lightning. It powers our economy and our military, as well as the machines that do much of the work that slaves have done in the past. So, one might argue that oil is wealth, strength, and freedom.

If those are not the holy trinity of our day, then what are?

Another important strategic advantage that Afghanistan provides is an inland air force base where planes and drones can land and refuel and take off again. If a good seaport was the most valuable infrastructure possession of empires prior to the 20th century, a good airport is the most valuable today.

Just as the Kabul River Valley and the Khyber Pass are the gateway to the Far East for Afghanistan, a military air base in Afghanistan is a gateway to the east for the United States and our allies. Bagram Air Field is the largest of such air bases in Afghanistan. It is located in a wide mountain valley, near Charikar, a city built on the foundations of one of Alexander's forts. At the intersection of several large rivers, the area offers a wide landing zone from the air and difficult access by land, since the roads leading to it must go through the mountains. If the US was to declare war on a country in the Middle East or Asia, or if we were to need a place to run or support covert operations, Bagram in Afghanistan is the higher ground from which the United States might stage an air attack.

The 164th MP Company deployed in March of 2011. Their plane landed at Bagram Airfield in Afghanistan. Part of their processing included additional IED training because that year had been one of the worst years for IED deaths in the war. The class was extensive. Trainers wanted soldiers to understand and follow protocol as thoroughly as possible. Their advice could minimize damage in an attack, and that could very well save some of their lives.

The 164th flew from there to Jalalabad, and then flew by helicopter to Mihtarlam, Laghman Province, in Eastern Afghanistan.

"It's the beginning of the fighting season," Enlow said. Most of the fighting happens in summer in Afghanistan, as winters are too harsh for the insurgency tactics of the Taliban. DOD casualty reports illustrate this same trend. In one graph, bars represent the monthly casualties. The tallest bars are consistently in June and July.

"Mihtarlam sits just out of the mountains," said Sgt. Enlow. "It sits in a kind of bowl or plain. The black hills is where we went to the range and on the other side of the black hills is actually where Alingar is."

The helicopters weaved their way through the wide mountain valleys and landed at Mihtarlam. The nervous, yet excited soldiers unloaded, bent over in the rotor wash.

Mihtarlam was known as a FOB, or Forward Operating Base. Soldiers slept in B-huts, or makeshift barracks. Hescos, large steel cages lined with durable fabric and filled with stone and sand, stood tall as barriers to enemy fire.

Hescos were and are the easiest way to build large walls for protection. A cheaper alternative to large concrete barriers, which were sometimes also used, they only required large amounts of dirt and stone, and a labor force. So, long before Devin arrived, soldiers used shovels and manpower or, if they were lucky, large machinery to fill the hescos.

"The hand-off procedure was probably ten days or better," estimated Enlow. "We did inventory and everything for the first few days; got all the equipment lined up, understood what we had. We went over trucks with the crews that got the trucks so we'd know any habitual discrepancies with that piece of equipment or whatever the case may be."

He was the first to go on patrols, riding along with the platoon that preceded them, learning how they conducted themselves, becoming familiar with the landscape. Then Enlow and the other Sergeants would take their own squads out, and have the other platoon's leaders sitting in the back seats, coaching them along.

"We signed for it after we took control of the mission and they stayed around, their leaders. All of our people came in pretty much in a couple days of each other. The leaders jumped right in and started getting oriented to the area with their platoons and would run missions."

It was a black-out FOB, which meant that no light was allowed that could be visible from any distance. When Devin and Stacey had to walk to go to the bathroom or go to the chow hall, they had to take a flashlight with a red lens.

Even the simplest things were colored with a hue of fear.

Their training took over. The leaders established routines, and the base became more familiar.

Guard towers stood nearly fifty feet high. Stacey and Devin both took their turns on guard duty, watching to be sure the gate was not breached.

Every Thursday night, though they weren't sure why, the FOB would take a lot of ineffective direct fire, or IDF, from the hills and mountains around the base. The insurgents would shoot rockets and rounds into the base from far off. Or they would hire or blackmail a local person to do it. Every day or two, Devin and the others would have to duck down into bunkers to avoid the IDF, but luckily there were many bunkers located at various points on base. To them, it was more of an annoyance than anything else. The insurgents could never hit anything important on the base, except once.

It was nighttime and everyone was lying down and getting ready to go to bed. Suddenly, a rocket flew over the walls of the base. It went over one truck, dipped between two others, and hit another, blowing through the doors. Fortunately, no one was in it and no one was hurt, but the wreckage of the truck served as a reminder to all of the soldiers on the FOB that they were in a live combat zone, no matter what anyone else called it, and that anything could happen.

Still, on the base, despite persistent Thursday night ineffective direct fire, Devin and Stacey had each other, a small piece of Western New York in Afghanistan, and the other soldiers had some of the conveniences of American life.

"We had plywood buildings," Stacey recalled, "but there were no windows. We had an air conditioner that worked half the time. The heat index would get up to 130 in the summer, so it was really hot and humid."

These modern conveniences were a blessing during the stifling heat and the long periods of waiting. Devin tried to keep in contact with family and friends back home.

"There wasn't really much to do at first," said Stacey. "They had this little computer lab that people donated. You could pay to get on the Internet for a set time."

"We emailed about every day and we Skyped maybe once a week," remembered Natasha, who would ask her about her time there and offer to send her care packages and any other subject that would help to keep Devin's mind off of where she was, even if only for a few minutes. It seemed to her that Devin didn't need much cheering up, however.

"She was happy to be there. She loved exactly what she did," said Natasha.

Stacey and Devin and the other young soldiers spent a lot of time on base, if they weren't on patrols.

"We pretty much had time to talk to everybody and hang out with everybody," said Stacey. "There were good days and bad days but for the most part on our down time we were hanging out and our whole platoon actually was pretty close."

"I didn't smoke myself but I'd always joke about how you smoke twelve packs a day because that's how you socialize with people," remarked Sgt. Enlow. "I'd stand around and shoot the

125

breeze and BS while they were smoking. Trying to be normal people in this hell-hole."

Even Devin, an avid runner, had picked up the smoking habit.

They would sometimes play soccer with the Jordanians, who were also stationed there.

"It was just us. Twenty, thirty of us," said Stacey Jordan.

One day, a care package arrived containing water guns and, inside the base, a group of them played war, using their combat training to soak each other in the hot sun.

Outside the wire, the border of the FOB, it was a culture shock for both Devin and Stacey. Popular media depictions of Afghanistan were generally similar to the Marvel action film *Ironman (2008)*, in which Tony Stark is captured by terrorists while selling weapons there. The Afghan characters, besides the doctor who helps Stark, are all depicted as rifle-carrying extremists.

The reality of Afghanistan, and the lives of the regular people there, would be completely unfamiliar to Devin and Stacey.

"It is a very poor country," said Stacey. "Where we were, there weren't any buildings like we would have here. Everything was made mostly out of cobb (mud bricks). A lot of dirt and sand. Trash everywhere. It's not developed like America."

The town where they were, Mihtarlam, is Persian for something like "Master Lam" or "Elder Lam." Lam is short for Lamech, the father of Noah, the famous ark-builder. Lamech was an ancestor of Abraham, and according to the Islamic faith, ancestor of Muhammad. There is even a shrine there, built inside a mosque that is reportedly atop Lamech's grave.

The main objective of patrols was to keep the peace in the area villages and to locate enemy insurgents or gather intelligence about them. The compact, single-story, square buildings were made of mud brick similar to the adobe style of the American southwest. The walls, plastered with clay, had timbers sticking out of the front of the flat roof. Sometimes a glass window, sometimes a wooden shutter left slightly ajar, or sometimes an open hole let in air and light. The homes were often arranged in square formations around a central courtyard. An adjacent building may be surrounded by a high stonewall, creating multiple courtyards, and compound boundaries. Sometimes canopies were strung up, or netting was draped over a high wood frame. In the Alingar River Valley, the buildings were set into the slope of the hill, like steps, one compound looking down into another and down from the higher ground toward the road below. Lower down the slope was a wide valley where a river flowed and crops grew. There the water gave life to many green fields, but higher up, above the highway, baked to a sandy color in the bright sun, the mud and stone houses blend in with the rocky hillsides.

The convoys tried to make their way down dirt paths, some of them washed out, or down narrow alleyways between compound walls.

"The majority of the time you couldn't get the vehicles in there," said Stacey.

The Sergeant would talk to the village elders through the interpreter, and they would build relationships with the locals. The American soldiers were obviously interested in any activity by Taliban or other insurgent forces in the area. They wanted to know if there had been any disruptions in the villagers' everyday lives or if there had been even any suspicious activity. In return, the Sergeant would ask if there was anything that they could do for them. Sometimes they would pull security for the area, but mostly, said Jordan, it was to "have them like us," or what was called "winning hearts and minds" in the US media.

"If they needed anything, we'd help them with it," said Stacey.

Stacey and Devin watched the locals make a specialty called "foot bread," which was simply a flat bread that is kneaded with the feet. They tried it and thought it wasn't bad, but they were not brave enough to fill the bread with any of the meat hanging in the warm, open-air shops.

Children constantly surrounded them, often staring. It must have been a culture shock for the children also, especially to see women soldiers. When the Taliban took over in the 1990s, women were not allowed to work outside of the house and all of the girls' schools in the country were closed. These children, who would have been born right around the US invasion, have seen many of those schools re-open, but in other areas of the country, the Taliban used violence and scare tactics to destroy girls' schools or intimidate families so that they would not send their daughters.[49] Women soldiers would have been entirely alien to many of them.

But the children's interest was more economic than cultural. Near Mihtarlam, they would beg soldiers for pens or bottles of water, anything that they could give. Anything with metal parts were popular because the local people would melt the metal down and make jewelry or crafts out of them. That, of course, made brass cartridge casings like gold to the children.

"That would be our entertainment," said Stacey. "Throwing them out to them."

Another surreal scene was a stray, three-legged dog that lived around one of the checkpoints. Every time a local Afghan would come by, the dog would growl, bark, and chase after him.

"It was crazy," reflected Stacey. "This little three-legged dog protecting us."

On patrols, they would listen to music by letting an iPhone's ear bud hang next to the microphone of a headset.

Missions were intermittent, but consistent. Every few days, every other day. Their overall mission was to train the Afghan National Police (ANP) so that they could eventually take over security duties. Many times this training would take place at an ANP police station, about 14 kilometers north of there in a village called Alingar, which was at the end of the Alingar River valley, a small tributary of the Kabul River.

"It was up in a valley away from Mihtarlam," said Sgt. Enlow. "Mihtarlam is set at a point of convergence for several bodies of water and several road ways. It's a natural place for a city in the seat of that province there. Alingar Valley was just one of many that shot up and away from the city of Mihtarlam."

The ANP station in Alingar was part of their squad's responsibility. They each had different precincts, but this was one that was shared between Enlow's squad and Brown's squad.

"Because of its location and complexity, we typically ran on that one together with a combined squad," said Enlow.

They would take the convoy on the road that parallels the river.

"You'd find one or two villages off of the main road that were next to a river or good body of water. Alingar kind of had both. Down in the valley there's a pretty significant river from Alingar Station. The stage surrounding Mihtarlam was very large as far as Afghan villages go. Very built up, but also very poor. Everything was based on agriculture. People selling camels, people selling instruments for farming... Water tied into that, so the river that came down into Alingar was very important for the people there."

A typical convoy for an excursion of that sort is usually four trucks with around sixteen passengers. The trucks were a mix of Humvees and Armored Security Vehicles (ASVs). In the truck is the driver, and the truck commander, or TC, which is usually the team leader. There is a rooftop turret gunner standing up and usually another person in the truck as an extra dismount.

Dismounting just means that some people get out of the truck and look around. Soldiers are trained to scan an area at five meters, twenty-five meters, and two hundred meters in order to be more observant. These 5-25-200 scans are needed when there may be hidden dangers that need closer inspection; however, not everyone in the truck will dismount. To provide cover, the gunner stays in the truck. The driver stays in the truck in case the vehicle needs to be moved, which also might provide cover or give the gunner a better vantage point.

This configuration was called "squad plus." A typical squad would be ten people. They would roll out with no fewer than fourteen.

"Unlike Iraq, where they would hit and run," said Enlow, "in Afghanistan they would now and then actually hit and fight so we had to run with a larger unit."

"We could do it all," said Enlow, describing the value of an MP unit. "We were armed with heavy armor like cavalry and we're generally more intelligent. We also get more training in dealing with non-combatants. We get more training dealing with relocation of prisoners of war and things like that. Maneuver commanders just like using us."

Dismounted patrols might go on for a mile, or maybe two miles. It gives the convoy a lot of eyes on the area, many soldiers looking out at many angles, and all of them talking via headsets, working together as one entity to accomplish the task and keep the squad safe.

If people stopped and talked, they would stop and talk. The interpreters likely spoke multiple languages, as Afghanistan has two official languages, Pashto and Dari. Pashto, with its roots in Arabic, is spoken mostly by Pashtuns. Dari is often called Afghan-Persian due to its roots in the Iranian language. It is spoken by the majority of Afghans and is mutually intelligible with modern Persian.

In interacting with the public with the help of an interpreter, Enlow concluded that most people in the area were just poor farmers trying to make a living.

"The indigenous people were generally supportive," he said.

The problem was that money would influence their decisions at times. A bribe from an insurgent might bring them more money than they'd make in five years.

"That's how they'd recruit people," said Enlow. "Some of the people who were facilitating some of the IED attacks were exploited indigenous people."

The local people were mostly Pashtun, the majority ethnic group in Afghanistan that spans the Afghanistan-Pakistan border, but areas around Kabul are also inhabited by Tajiks, the second largest ethnic group in the country.

"Taliban and Al-Qaeda wanted to come in and fight the western power they saw as an invading force," said Enlow. "There was a definite pushback at times because they weren't getting what they wanted."

Navigating and responding to enemy pushback while evading innumerable other obstacles was the challenge. From the driver's perspective, even with training, the vehicles can be difficult to get used to because of the poor visibility, especially on the passenger side of the truck. So the driver had to rely a lot on the gunner and the truck commander to clear obstacles on that side.

This made the already dangerous roads more dangerous. There were narrow passages, open areas with no cover, even IED blast sites, giant craters in the asphalt.

The patrols look for anything out of place, though how they are supposed to spot that sort of thing is beyond imagination. They look for disturbances in the soil, piles of debris, or seams in the roadway where recent repairs had taken place. Anything that looks different than the last patrol.

They would usually stop before crossing a creek bed, or *wadi*, and dismount. The wadis typically went under the road, through a culvert. Looking through the scope of the gun, they could see far uphill and downhill along the course of the wadi. If everything looked good, they would cross the culvert.

In an area where needed for security, the convoy commander would stop the convoy and order a dismount. According to first hand sources, this was done about ninety percent of the time. It wasn't always necessary to dismount, and it didn't guarantee that an IED would be found. In fact, dismounted patrols left the convoy open not only to sniper fire but also to any other form of projectile, be it a rock or a rocket-propelled grenade. Nevertheless, that was the job.

So they would stop and get out, check the angles. All eyes, every direction. Report back.

Dangerous areas were not hard to recognize, but it was impossible to say that anywhere outside the wire was safe. Every day, when those convoys rolled out, it was very possible that they would not all return.

It took the better part of an hour to ride up to the Alingar area and they generally would stay a night, or two nights, and then they would come back. They would take enough supplies to get by for two to three days, but it was never longer than that. After that they would need to return to base and get re-fit, or re-supplied with food, water, clothes, and fuel.

While there, the American soldiers focused on illustrating policing methods.

"We showed them our procedures. We taught them how to arrest people. We helped to teach them how to shoot," said Stacey.

They also would go on patrols with the Afghani police, and the Afghanis would show them how they operate. After a short time, it became clear to Stacey that there were not a lot of rules.

"I never really got to talk to them. That was more the higher-ups. I would pretty much just pull security while they talked," she explained. "But from what I've seen and what I've heard, they don't really have many rules."

On one occasion, a young boy was accused of stealing. There was no formal arrest and no sentencing. He was publicly beaten.

"They just kept explaining that it was their way of doing things and that there was nothing that we could do about it."

They had to stand back let it happen.

"They didn't beat him to death or anything," she said, but she could tell the boy was in pain.

This custom may have been exercised as part of what is known as *pashtunwali*, or the unwritten codes of honor among the Pashtuns. One part of *pashtunwali* is Badal, or retaliation. It is essential for a Pashtun to retaliate against those who have wronged him or else be shamed and lose honor and dignity.[50]

Unable to communicate and confronted with cultural norms that were unlike their own, it was difficult at times for Snyder, Jordan, and the others to distinguish between the local tribes, the Taliban, and Arabs. It made the peacekeeping effort that much more nerve-wracking. A soldier could scan a city courtyard and imagine the enemy everywhere.

On Stacey Jordan's first mission, a sniper was active. He shot out the window of the first truck in her convoy, but luckily there were no injuries.

Another patrol was just after Pastor Terry Jones, Preacher for the Christian Dove World Outreach Center in Gainesville, Florida publicly burned the Koran on March 20, 2011.[51] Afghan President Hamid Karzai denounced the burning and the resulting protests turned to riots in the Afghan city Mazar-i-Sharif. 27 UN employees were killed as a result between April 1 and April 5th, 2011.[52]

Stacey Jordan remembers being in the truck and seeing buildings and car tires on fire. Rioters filled the streets, even in their small city, surrounding their convoy.

"We were stuck on the road for over four hours because there was just hundreds of them blocking the road, not letting us go," she said. "I was nervous. There was a bunch of angry people and some setting off these little cherry bombs, like fire crackers. You don't know if it's an actual shooting. It was scary. It was very frustrating, but we couldn't do anything."

It was a difficult mission in an area that was hard to patrol. Most locations that they could access were along the highway. Populated areas tended to have buildings both up-slope and down-slope from the convoy, making the convoy vulnerable from two sides. Since there was only one highway, it was impossible to go anywhere quickly, and because the likelihood of an attack on that highway was great, that meant that patrols needed to dismount frequently in order to keep the convoy secure. If they did not dismount, they moved very slowly through any area that made them vulnerable to attack.

"It's a constant battle of waking up every morning and getting ready to go out on a mission and you're always wondering, 'Am I going to make it home today?'" explained Josh Pruitt, a soldier in their platoon. "You had to do that every day."

Part 3: Suffering

"I have died before dying,
through my woes…"
         --Euripides, *Hecuba*

Chapter 10: Recognition

It was not long after the hand off that the 164th MP Company in Mihtarlam became aware of just how dangerous things could be. On April 6, 2011 Sgt. Brown's squad went out on patrol and their truck was hit by an IED. Three people were in the truck. The gunner, a private, was thrown from the turret and paralyzed. The others had shrapnel injuries and the sergeant was medically retired.

It was an eye opener for some.

"The guys, we would call them *cherry*," said Enlow, "were walking around kind of wide-eyed like 'Oh shit what did I get myself into.' The veterans were like 'Well, we got into a hot zone. We know what's coming.' We just kind of suck it in like 'Well, crap.'"

He knew that the war was on. The enemy was present, and they were using known IED tactics. The awareness of that fact changed the tone of the mission for many people in the platoon. Enlow had been to Iraq, where IEDs were being hidden in yellow plastic cooking oil jugs, in trash piles, or on the backside of guardrails. He understood the threats.

"You kind of get to that point where everything's a bomb," said Enlow. "It's just whether or not it's my time."

The Army has tried to address the problem of explosive ordnance disposal (EOD) since WWII, when land mines were extensively used. EOD was created as a joint service program at that time and for most of the EODs existence the Navy has managed training. Today, Army EOD personnel train at Eglin Naval School. Their purpose is to mitigate IED hazards and ensure that soldiers understand the trends in explosive ordnance usage.

It's a good thing they do. Improvised explosive devices (IEDs) and explosively formed penetrators (EFPs) have become an increasingly popular tool of insurgency, especially against "softer military targets such as Humvees, trucks, and foot patrols."[53] They are cheap to make and effective against an undoubtedly superior military force. The difference between the two types of ordnance is that the IED creates a large blast and an EFP punches a "teardrop" of molten metal through the armored vehicle. Both can be detonated in a variety of ways, though they are most frequently set off by cell phone signal or command wire.

Response to this emerging military reality by "the Big Army" has been to provide additional training, provide EOD support and intelligence at each forward operating base, and to use EOD crews to sweep entire stretches of highway in hot zones. This has resulted in expenditures of "$17 billion on various anti-IED gear over the last decade, and that's not counting the $45 billion we've spent on mine-resistant vehicles," writes Peter W. Singer for the Brookings Institute in 2012.

The Pentagon ordered these sales based on the research of the Joint IED Defeat Organization (JIEDDO), which was set up to "rapidly sort through and acquire technology to help troops find IEDs on the battlefield."[54] Their three priorities were to "Attack the Network, Defeat the Device, and Train the Force." Defeating the device included using some new technology like various kinds of metal detectors, backpack radio jammers such as the THOR, EOD robots, and other vehicle-mounted counter-IED equipment. Training the force meant training them to use those devices as well as changes in tactics in order to avoid IED attacks. One priority is summarized in a JIEDDO pamphlet entitled "Dismounted Operations in an IED Environment" from 2006. It describes how dismounted operations, or "military operations on foot," are being made safer by the new gear.

The accounts of surgeons at Bagram and those of medically retired soldiers might offer a different picture. In her sobering work *They Were Soldiers*, Ann Jones tells of the overworked surgeons who routinely perform multiple major surgeries each day on individuals injured by IEDs. Multiple doctors are sometimes required to stabilize a soldier. Many times amputations are required due to massive leg wounds, as well as dirt and debris in the wounds. Jones, a long time foreign correspondent in Afghanistan, calls these injuries "signatures" of the war in Afghanistan.

"This war now is mostly about explosions," she wrote.

Despite the measured tactical response to the proliferations of IEDs by the military as a whole, the response of the soldiers has more similarity to rolling dice or playing roulette. Although still following protocol, they are keenly aware that some of these tactics might not work, and that some of them are too cumbersome to carry out if they are to complete their assigned missions. The very definition of being a soldier is to expose oneself to a great danger, and soldiers understand this better than anyone, that they are vulnerable to attack even as they follow protocol to minimize that vulnerability. There is no guarantee of safety.

"There are always different opinions on how to address anything," said Enlow. "One guy that you work for would want you to just haul balls everywhere you went. That was his defense against it. You screw up their timing if you're just hauling ass. There was another guy that wanted you to go slow and methodical and peek under everything or shoot it with an M4 to make sure it wasn't going to blow up."

Every object was a potential bomb, and everything and everyone was a potential threat. Thrust into chaos and hostility, it was enough to break some of the soldiers.

"I mean a lot of guys would just turn into stress balls and couldn't handle it or were scared shitless every time they busted the wire," said Enlow.

"Generally the rest of us just refused to live in fear. I'm going to do my job and if I see something that's suspicious I'm going to act accordingly but I'm not going to be afraid of anything."

About a month after the initial IED attack, on May 1, 2011, US Special Forces raided a large, high-walled compound in Abbottabad, Pakistan in the middle of the night and killed the aging but elusive Al Qaeda leader Osama bin Laden.[55]

"The death of Bin Laden marks the most significant achievement to date in our nation's effort to defeat Al Qaeda," said President Obama, in an address to the nation, just hours later. "But his death does not mark the end of our effort. There's no doubt that Al Qaeda will continue to pursue attacks against us. We must and we will remain vigilant at home and abroad."[56]

This probably reflected the opinion of many US soldiers deployed at the time. It was the case for Enlow and the others. While happy to see one of the original goals of the GWOT finally attained after ten years, the troops in Devin's platoon kept their focus on their own mission.

They continued routine training missions, trying to defend against IEDs by projecting a tough image.

"Look like a hard target," said Enlow. "Look like a guy they don't want to mess with. If you look like you're going to eff them up after you get hit, they might pass you up."

Jeremy Johnson, another soldier in their platoon, remembers the difficulty of looking like a "hard target" in the Afghan landscape. One of the ways that our soldiers are vulnerable is that insurgents hide among civilians. The villages, then, offer cover.

"I remember it [a local village] is on the side of a hill. Part of it is on the hill and part is below the hill and the road goes up midway up the hill. So as you're driving down the road you got houses and buildings higher than you and buildings lower than you."

Tactically, that kind of terrain puts our convoys at a distinct disadvantage. Going through those villages, on the only roads that will allow their large vehicles to pass, our convoys are funneled into traps. The only solution, dismounted patrol, means exposure to enemy fire.

"The way I looked at it, even though I wound up getting injured in Iraq," said Enlow, "was if it's meant to be, it's meant to be."

Given these circumstances, some soldiers turned to prayer. Written on the inside of one of the M-ATVs was "Galacians 6:18." The passage from the King James Bible reads: "Brethren, the grace of our Lord Jesus Christ be with your spirit. Amen."

The truth is that there is no known 100% defense against an IED. There are ways of minimizing the impact, such as the v-hull construction of the newest trucks. These vehicles, called mine-resistant ambush-protected (MRAPs), are safer because their design deflects the blast away from the troops. It has probably saved hundreds of lives, if not thousands, to date. Unfortunately, it was only developed in 2008, so the initial order was not on the ground in

Afghanistan until October 2009.[57] The response of the insurgents was to build bigger and better bombs. IEDs became stronger and EFPs became more prevalent, due to their armor piercing capacity.

Multiple orders were filled after that, including one in February 2011 for over 2,000 for underbody improvement kits (UIKs), which added extra armor beneath the vehicles. They would not be delivered until September 2011.[58] Other similar improvements were made to military vehicles like the Stryker, an eight-wheeled truck, which was upgraded to include a double v-hull. These vehicles were just being made available to Stryker units near Kandahar right around the time of Devin Snyder's deployment.[59]

Back home, friends and family were sheltered from the realities that soldiers were facing in Mihtarlam.

"We knew that it wasn't necessarily an okay place," said Danette. "But from every impression that I got from Dineen, she was in a place where she was reasonably safe. Unbeknownst to us, she was actually going out on different patrols."

Her husband Greg took a different approach.

"If I don't think about this, it'll be okay," he reasoned. "I won't even worry about it. If I put it out of my mind, everything will be okay. What are the chances? I'm not even going to think about it. What the hell is she going to do? Where are they going to put her? They're not going to put this little girl in the front."

"I was thinking she's not going to leave the base," said Danette. "She's got to stay there."

"What are the odds?" said Greg. "She's going to be home. We'll wake up and she'll be home and her deployment's done. That was my attitude."

Friends stayed in contact through Facebook. Devin was already making plans for when she returned, so she could look forward to something.

"It was actually a couple days before she died we were talking on Facebook," said Meaghan Oas. "She was so excited to come home, she couldn't wait. She had a shopping trip planned with her mom. So we were trying to make plans for when we could catch up and see each other."

Shopping at the mall with mom was not the only plan. Devin told Dineen that she would like to get ahold of Jessica Jeffords again. The two had had a sort of falling out, but Devin was reassessing that. Through Dineen, the two had plans to meet in New York in July 2011, when Devin would be home on leave. The Thursday before she was killed, Dineen and Devin spoke.

"I've got to get a hold of Jessica and see if she's still coming," said Devin. "Can you get ahold of Jessica for me?"

"Yeah, absolutely," said Dineen. "I can contact her and let her know you still want that because I think she still thinks that you're mad."

"Yeah, I want her there," said Devin. "Make sure you tell Jessica when you talk to her that we're going to go the Buffalo mall."

After the day's work on June 3rd, 2011, Devin Snyder and Stacey Jordan would hang out the exact way that any two, young, female roommates would after work. They would get cleaned up, get dressed, talk, and listen to music. Then they went to eat together. That night at dinner, they were both excited that they were both going to have the next day off. The mood was light, and there was a sense of relief.

"We finally get the whole day off," Devin said excitedly that night. They had only seen each other recently in passing, between shifts and at bedtime. Now their hearts were set on having a whole day to just relax and hang out. To be normal.

After showers, they came back to the barracks and Devin's squad leader, Sgt. Brown showed up. He said that they needed to go to a briefing. At the briefing, orders were that Enlow's squad (plus a few extra) were going out on patrol the next day after all. Sgt. Brown was leaving for Bagram to interview for an application to Officer Candidate School.

"The two days before we were scheduled as the Quick Reaction Force (QRF)," recalled Jeremy Johnson. "So on June 4th we were supposed to have gotten a call to leave to Jalalabad but for some reason that mission got canceled and the lieutenant asked Sergeant Enlow to put a team together and go up to Alingar district. He decided to use the same manifest as two days before which put me, Sgt. Bell, Spec. Voakes and Sgt. Snyder into the front truck."

142

When Devin came back from the briefing, she was furious. It was supposed to have been her first day off in what seemed like forever, and she had been looking forward to the down time. In that situation, it is clear that any time spent in the relatively safe confines of the base would be profoundly less stressful than going on patrols. In the same way that rest is important for a civilian workforce, soldiers need that downtime in order to manage the stress of being in a combat zone. In Afghanistan, they would get less downtime because they always needed larger convoys.

Devin, Stacey, and Sgt. Christopher Bell were sitting around on the steps to their building, talking and making light of the situation. Bell and Snyder were in the same squad, so they both knew that they were not going to be on base the next day. But something was not right. They all knew it. Bell and Snyder noticed that the lineup of the trucks were such that three team leaders were in one truck. Usually, it is procedure to split up the team leaders, perhaps as TCs or truck commanders, since they have more experience and are also responsible for the other soldiers. In addition, a Dyncorp civilian contractor named Brett Benson was in the front truck.

Bell and Snyder couldn't help but be cynically amused.

"What if something did happen?" one of them said.

"They'd lose three team leaders at once."

Jordan, sensing the underlying uneasiness, spoke up.

"Guys! Don't joke about this. It's not cool."

The subject was changed, but there was still a strange feeling all that night. Stacey couldn't sleep. Devin couldn't sleep. So they stayed up, talking. Stacey recalled feeling that "something was about to happen."

They passed the hours going out for cigarettes, talking, then walking to the chow hall for some muffins. But they still couldn't sleep.

"You guys talking about that shit made my heart sink," Stacey told Devin.

Her Facebook post that night was "Thinking about too much."

At some point that night, Sgt. Enlow told the interpreter to be at the trucks at 08:45.

The next morning, Stacey went to see Devin and her squad off. It was part of their daily routine. If Stacey was going out, Devin would come down and see her off, or vice versa. They'd talk for a little bit, then say I love you, have a last cigarette, and then say see you later. But the day Devin went on that mission, they did not follow their routine. Stacey was up early and at the truck line, cleaning their trucks, when Devin and the others came down to set up their own trucks and do inspections.

Devin just wasn't the same that day. Sleep deprived and depressed, she kept to herself quietly.

"Wanna cigarette?" asked Stacey, trying to break through.

"Nope," she said, shortly, not interested in speaking to anyone. She just sat by herself on a cement barrier and waited. There was a heavy mood hanging in the air that whole morning. Devin didn't want to do their daily routine.

"It was a really strange day," remembered Stacey. "Devin wasn't acting like herself. I should have just gone over to her and said 'I love you' like every other day, but because of the way she was acting, I didn't. She didn't want anyone to talk to her. But I wish I had. I think about it all the time, and I regret it every day."

It was strange. Stacey stayed on base all day. She just sat there by herself. No one was talking anyway. Something wasn't right. Stacey had a bad feeling and she thought Devin felt it too. It was a feeling like someone was condemned, but they didn't know who, or for what crime.

Chapter 11: The Enemy's Vote[60]

"We had gotten into our own rhythm," remembered Enlow. They knew a threat was present, and they knew the hot spots. Missions would come in the preceding day, some a week in advance. Squad leaders would hash out the troop assignments, seat assignments, and truck layouts.

On June 4, Sgt. Enlow conducted safety briefings and ensured that the team leaders were getting through Pre-Combat Checks (PCCs) and Pre-Combat Inspections (PCIs) with the soldiers. These extensive checks include the inspection of personal gear, communications equipment, patrol vehicles, several kinds of first aid kits, weapons, and more.[61]

"There's an enormous amount of detail that goes into any combat mission like that," he remembered. "We had just gotten into a rhythm where we could get it done and get out. I did the group ticket, I had to turn it in to the TOC (tactical operations center) so they would know who's going, where we're going, what time we're supposed to be going, when we should be back in contact. All that was done."

Devin met most of the others in their convoy at the vehicle line at 0800 to do maintenance checks and load gear. All gear and equipment was functioning properly, including the standard issue Counter-IED jammers in all of the vehicles. The soldiers attended to their own trucks. As the convoy's rear gunner loaded the 4th truck with water and MREs, Jeremy Johnson heard there was going to be a change.

"So that morning I set the truck up," said Jeremy Johnson, "and about thirty minutes to forty-five minutes before we report to roll out the gate, Sgt. Bell came up and told me that Sgt. Enlow moved me into his truck, the second truck."

As the team leaders led the troops through their battle drills, including IED response, Sgt. Enlow went to get the most recent intelligence brief. He was told that there were "several things going on in the surrounding valleys in Lahgman" including "several IED threats." He was told of a specific IED threat, near a specific location, perhaps in a recently rebuilt culvert. He took notes on the threats in order to plot their location in the convoy's navigation equipment and returned to the truck line to give the soldiers a briefing of the day's activities.

At about this time, the Afghani interpreter showed up, and Enlow started his briefing.

The mission was simple. They would ride northeast up a valley into the mountains to Alingar District Center (DC) to "conduct Afghan National Police (ANP) mentorship in the form of individual movement techniques training, reacting to contact, and conducting a dismounted patrol with the ANP south of Alingar." This valley had only one major road along the west side and the road ended only 22km away, at Alingar, their destination. It was a straight line through an area where there had been several previous IED attacks, but it was a mission that they had done many times before.

"Even though we do this mission on a regular basis, we can't get complacent," Enlow said. "We need to be extra diligent around the threat areas." He told them about the possibility of IEDs and suicide bombers in the area. Records show that they were instructed on "how to react to small arms, sniper fire, indirect fire, what to do if we got hit by an IED."

"We loaded up, double-checked our supplies to make sure we had what we needed, and headed out," said Enlow.

The convoy left the base at Mihtarlam at about 10:15am. Contrary to the news reports, in the lead vehicle were five people: Sgt. Powell in the front passenger seat, Cpl. Bell driving, Spec. Devin Snyder in the rear passenger seat, PFC Voakes standing in the gunner's turret, and Brett Benton, a private military contractor for Dyncorp in the rear driver's seat.

Benton was a police officer in northern Kentucky for more than a decade. He started the K9 program in Kenton County, KY, a county that borders the city of Cincinnati, OH. Dyncorp International, now owned by Delta Tucker Holdings, Inc., received Pentagon contracts in 2005, 2010, and 2015 to "provide advisory, training and mentoring services" to the Afghanistan National Police and the Afghanistan National Army.[62] Benton was part of that effort.

On the way, one of the gunners reported that they "stopped at a few previous blast sites and encountered no IEDs or hostile enemy forces."

One soldier, a medic, said, "at every previous blast site we slowed down and checked for IEDs."

Another soldier, a passenger in one of the rear driver's side seats, reported that "there was extra emphasis put toward the checking of the culverts and wadis for IEDs" and that they were reminded "not to become complacent."

At about 10:25am, they stopped at a culvert that had recently been rebuilt.

"We performed a security halt," said another soldier.

"We had been notified in the mission brief that there was an IED placed at a particular grid mark," said another soldier. They dismounted, looked for signs of IEDs, but found that it was clear, and drove on.

"Once we busted the wire it was a typical day," said Enlow. "We stopped at one point because there had been a hot spot for I.E.D.s. We did a dismounted check of the area, mounted back up, pushed forward out towards Alingar."

"The convoy stopped to check a culvert that was damaged for possible IEDs," said Johnson in his statement. "The TC of the truck moved to the driver seat and moved me to the TC seat. The driver moved to the back right seat."

"I was removed from driving because Enlow was sick," said another member of their squad. "Sgt. Enlow said he was going to drive so I became a passenger and I sat behind the TC seat and Johnson became the TC."

"As I was getting into the truck," said Johnson, "I looked over to Snyder and said something to her that made her laugh and that was the last thing I saw of her. Her smiling."

"I put Jeremy up in the TC seat and I drove for him just because that's how we teach people," explained Sgt. Enlow. "I was still in control of the truck. He wasn't making any significant calls, but he was seeing what it was like to be there running the maps and our system."

147

"I was manning the blue force tracker which was the computer system that tracks almost all the vehicles in the theater through GPS," said Johnson. "I was being the back and forth from Sgt. Enlow to the TOCs."

The convoy approached an intersection, continued while scanning for devices, then "proceeded through the area without incident."

Back on the road, heading north to Alingar District Center, the convoy was going pretty fast. Enlow later reported that the team was "focused on mission." Someone from behind called out to slow down, since they were approaching the Village of Kanda, which was also the site of a previous IED attack.

"We drove through the countryside. Along the side toward the black hills. It seemed as though we had two or three other stops," reported one of the soldiers.

The convoy arrived at the village about thirty minutes after leaving base. Slowly moving along, at about 10:40am, they arrived at the former blast site.

"As we entered the village," reported one soldier, "the lead vehicle slowed to a stop to check a previous blast hole that has been used on several occasions in the past."

"I don't remember hearing anyone say the hole was clear," reported the medic, who was in the third truck.

They paused for a moment, checking the hole, soldiers inside the lead truck were doing 5-25-200 scans, the gunner looked closely for a glint of wire, a disturbance in the dirt, or anything protruding. Perhaps they were mesmerized by the large crater left by the previous blast and maybe paralyzed for a moment with the memory of what had happened before. There was a long silent moment.

They did not dismount as they had at the culvert. The lead truck rolled forward, turning to the left, around the hole.

"We vary our TTPs on how we clear so as not to set a pattern," reported another soldier. "It is left to the discretion of lead TC to make the decision of whether to dismount or scan [in order to] avoid setting a pattern. If we dismount every time, the enemy could easily start putting landmines in the wadi/fields." This would leave them exposed to landmines because to clear a bottleneck site they would have to patrol out to 250 meters.

"If the first truck wanted to do a dismount we would have done a dismount," said Sgt. Enlow. "I told them I trusted their point."

"I empowered my junior leaders to think about that on their own and come up with a decision on what they wanted to do," said Enlow. "Not because I'm a pussy and couldn't make the decision, but my duty in life was to train the next batch of leaders."

Then, like a lightning strike from below, the IED went off as the lead truck was turning around the hole. Instantly, there was a cloud of dust and flying debris.

"I heard a loud BOOM," said the medic.

"The blast went off under the truck, sending it maybe twenty—it seems thirty feet in the air but there's no way," remembered Sgt. Enlow, who was in the second truck. "Between ten, twenty feet up in the air. So much so that the bottom of the MV was pushed in several feet."

"When the IED went off," remembered Johnson, "it blew the truck about 50 feet in the air and rotated the truck probably from 12 o'clock closer to about 10 o'clock and moved it about 15 feet over. It was massive."

Those in the second truck could feel, and even see, the shock wave hit them.

After a short pause left in the wake of the shock wave, someone yelled "IED! IED! IED!" over the radio.

In the third truck, the Aid and Litter vehicle, the gunner, fearful of being pinned down and attacked, started yelling in the headset at the rear vehicle.

"Back up! Back up!"

"Calm down!" said the medic. "Are you okay?"

"Back up! Back up!"

"Shut the hell up!" she said. "You kicked the switch! Turn the headset back on!"

"DISMOUNT! DISMOUNT! DISMOUNT!"

Despite the panic of one, the gunners held to their fields of fire, "scanning for a trigger man or the possibility of an oncoming ambush."

In the rear truck, the gunner had their backs.

"I stopped anyone from coming up on the convoy's six and kept the people on foot back as well. The local nationals all kicked back about 75-100 meters. Dyncorp [personnel] aided as my backup on the ground," reported the rear gunner.

"I called over the radio to get a status on the disabled truck. No response."

5-25-200 meter scans were completed by the whole convoy. All was clear. There was no sign of anything at close range, at 200 meters, someone witnessed civilians running scared.

"I dismounted and checked under the truck for any possible IEDs," reported one soldier. "I noted nothing under our truck, so I tactically made my way up to the hit truck, checking under vehicles and between buildings and roofs along the way, working to make sure our rear was guarded and secure."

"I scanned my sector around the 9 o'clock and saw only a few local nationals in the distance," said another soldier, a gunner. "However I do believe I saw a local national recording us. I was not sure if he had a camera in his hand or not due to his distance... I did not have binoculars in the turret with me... the only thing I know is that it was not a weapon."

Multiple soldiers then reported two males running away down the wadi. No weapons were seen by the gunner, though another soldier reported seeing one. They could not confirm weapons nor that they were in fact the trigger men for the IED.

"Do not engage," said Sgt. Enlow. "They could just be scared locals."

Rules of engagement were that soldiers needed to be certain that the target was a legitimate military threat.

After the rest of the convoy began to dismount, the two local nationals were gone.

"Every fiber of our being wanted to level that whole village," said Enlow. "But we knew that by doing so we would just create more insurgents."

Dismounted soldiers set up security 360 degrees around the blast, checking for secondary IEDs, making sure it was clear to start first aid.

"I saw my buddies laying outside the truck," said one soldier as he made his way to a pile of rocks near a wall to pull security. "I could not make out who was who."

"There were people near the buildings, in the shaded area," reported another soldier. "[They were] caught in an attack… They did not show any action of hostility, but fear."

Another soldier pulled security down the wadi then was sent "to secure an open field and hold security on it to give the birds an area to land." A medevac request was sent.

Down an alleyway, behind the shops, Johnson saw 30 men and many children hiding.

As security was established, the Aid and Litter team was called out. They had readied the aid bags previously. A typical aid and litter kit includes necessary combat medical items, such as tourniquets, gauze and field dressing, an airway tube, HyFin chest seal (which is like a large sticker or patch to put over a chest wound), a fold-up litter (lightweight stretcher) and ratchet strap, a body bag, and a casualty equipment bag. Now, while the driver and gunner remained in her truck, the medic ran out to the blast site.

"The entire right side of the vehicle was blown off," she reported.

"The trucks are literally coming apart when hit with IEDs," said another soldier.

"I dismounted to evaluate casualties," said a soldier on the driver's side. "Brett Benton was pulled out of the vehicle. He didn't have a pulse. Corporal Bell was next but he was stuck between the seat and the dashboard. [There were] severe injuries to his thighs."

One soldier worked on getting Benton onto a litter.

The medic yelled for another aid bag. Johnson left security and ran to the truck to get the bag.

CPL Bell didn't have a pulse. Then the medic moved on to Snyder who had been pulled out. One soldier found Devin Snyder

151

"hanging from the truck by her seat belt because her seat wasn't there."

He unbuckled her, carried her a couple feet away, and laid her down on the ground.

"I found no signs of life," he reported.

He applied a tourniquet to Devin's left leg, but she was still "unresponsive." He could not find a pulse.

The second truck moved to lead position. Their gunner took over the 12 o'clock vector. Johnson ran to get the medic another WALK kit (Warrior Aid and Litter Kit).

PFC Voakes was found alive, ten feet from truck, thrown from gunner's station. He had a weak pulse and shallow breathing.

"We began first aid on PFC Voakes. We applied two tourniquets to PFC Voakes and then [the medic] began to apply an oral airway device to assist PFC Voakes in breathing."

It was a medic's worst nightmare. There was almost nothing she could do. She began ordering others to help her.

"Do what you learned and apply a tourniquet where you see bleeding or laceration!"

Then she came back to Voakes. She cut his shirt off and checked for wounds. Another soldier lifted him onto the litter while she held his head in place. They strapped him in, "got him packaged for transport," and moved him to the landing zone (LZ).

"After that I went back to SPC Snyder and tried to feel for a pulse," said the medic, unwilling to accept it. "I thought I felt a slight pulse but I think it may have been my own pulse or just adrenaline pumping because I don't think anyone else felt that pulse, so I tried to conduct CPR on her and [there was] no response."

"Everyone, except Voakes, had suffered from circulatory system failure from the blast," said Enlow. "This was apparent to me from the absence of bleeding from the wounds that would normally produce large volumes of easily observed blood."

Medevac updated the request and sent out for three KIA and one WIA.

Sgt. Powell had been ejected, and was found far from vehicle by security.

"I began checking his pulse and breathing, looking for any signs of life," reported one soldier. "I found neither... I noticed severe trauma to the top of his head and realized that there was nothing that I could do for him."

The Medevac request was updated to include Powell, KIA.

"They all had traumatic brain injuries... cause of death was internal bleeding," reported the medic.

"There was a dingo cart that was approximately 20 feet from the blast that turned into the creek area," reported one of the soldiers. "The interpreter got out of the truck and asked him if he was okay."

Soldiers securing the farm field threw a purple smoke grenade to mark the landing zone. At 11:16, about 30 minutes after the IED blast, helicopters arrived to medevac Voakes. He was loaded up, then Snyder, Bell, and Benton. They rushed to Jalalabad Airfield to get Voakes the attention he needed.

Because there was not enough room in the medevac for all of the deceased, Sgt. Powell was secured in a litter and body bag and stowed away in the shade to wait for the next medevac.

The soldiers spent the time gathering gear, weapons, and sensitive items from the area, so that insurgents could not use those things against our own troops. The sun was getting hotter.

"All I was able to do was pull security for our rear and toss water to my comrades on the ground from the cooler in our truck," reported the rear gunner. "A huge convoy... rolled up behind me, so I changed my sector of fire and a wrecker was called up to haul away the wreckage of the truck after the blast."

Many of the others continued pulling security until water was depleted.

The Quick Reaction Force (QRF) showed up and took over security.

"So at this point we were able to relax, find some shade, get some water and come together as a squad," reported Enlow.

"It was a while in a shaded area I pulled guard and drank water for a time when I was told to go back to the truck before I became a heat casualty," said one soldier.

Another soldier walked around the truck, picking up pieces and placing them in a pile. A few of the trucks were sent back to base. The QRF worked on loading the truck onto a flatbed using a mechanical arm. The convoy commanders spoke while their soldiers kept watch.

EOD arrived and an investigation of the area uncovered "one copper command detonation wire buried and running east down the wadi...at the three o'clock position along the rock wall."

They waited a long time. The interpreter fell asleep in the truck and was shaken awake.

"We were out there for quite some time," said Enlow. "We had to do sub-divided inventory and make sure all the weapons and radios and navigation equipment and everything that could be considered sensitive was accounted for and loaded up...Then you've got the decision that has to be made about how to get your guys out of there. What's going to happen with the vehicle, what are you doing with this, how are you getting everybody back. We got loaded up... We had to drive back. We weren't going to get flown out of there..."

All the trucks that were there fell in line and became part of that convoy.

"We were spent, tired, hurt [from] losing our friends," one soldier reported.

Riding back to the FOB was silent and somehow cold.

"The weather was hot, but it was cold," said Johnson. "Numb, I guess."

The date, 6/4/11, had not been a good day for the 164th.

They rode onward to the FOB, outward from the center of the explosion, like the first wave of ever-expanding concentric circles of grief.

Enlow tried his best to rationalize it: "There's no way you would see it. There could be a perfectly finished road on top of it and you wouldn't spot it unless you were sweeping the area just for that. We had counter-I.E.D. crews that swept that very road on a regular basis. I don't know what the window was between the last counter-I.E.D. sweep but they would see those trucks come through and go 'okay, now we plant it because they're not going to catch it.' Then the next convoy coming through goes 'oh, the counter-I.E.D. crew was through here yesterday. It should be relatively clear.' It was a crapshoot. We weren't fighting stupid people. We were fighting tacticians."

Back on base, Enlow debriefed the group. Since he had more experience in combat than many of them, he felt like he could offer them guidance, even as he grieved himself. First, wanting to be upfront and honest, he told them that Voakes had died.

"He wasn't stable enough to do surgery. His injuries were too great," said Enlow.

After letting that set in for a minute, he continued.

"At the end of the day we're not in control of everything a hundred percent of the time, but I'm proud of you. You all did very well and held your shit together better than some units would ever dream of. I'm proud of every single one of you."

He also warned that they should not internalize their grief. Recognizing the long-term problems associated with PTSD, Enlow was instituting a sort of early intervention therapy. He demanded that they talk to each other, or they would not make it through their deployment.

"It doesn't matter if it's your friend, your squad leader, your boss; it could be anybody. The way we get through this and do this is by talking to each other. It's as simple as 'I'm sad my teammates, my brothers, my sisters, are not with us anymore.' 'I'm mad at you because I think you could have done this better' that's absolutely okay. We need to be able to say those things and not worry about repercussions."

"I reiterated that all that were lost were phenomenal soldiers and I was proud to be in the army with them in that platoon," said Enlow. "Then we broke from there."

"After the debriefing," reported one soldier, "I went and shut myself in my room to read my Bible and pray."

Later, the platoon Sergeant pulled everyone who had remained on the FOB together and explained what had happened.

"One of the trucks got hit by an IED," he said. "And they all didn't make it."

They started naming off names.

The second wave of grief washed over them.

"I lost it," said Stacey.

"It was a little hard because a lot of them wanted to know what happened," said Johnson, who was trying to deal with his own sadness and anger. "Almost instantly of being back we were asked what happened and who did what."

It was a time in the war when the insurgents had the most firepower and the NATO convoys had little defense. 2009, 2010, and 2011 were the three years with the highest number of IED fatalities in Afghanistan. Devin was the first female soldier from New York State to die in Afghanistan.

"It was still my mission," said Enlow. "I was the one that was in control calling the shots. It was my mission, it was my day. I made the trip ticket; I put the people in the vehicles. That decision lost the lives of five people."

Josh Pruitt and others were not at Mihtarlam on that day. They were at Jalalabad Air Field being trained to drive the new MaxxPros. It was a forty-hour course. On the last day, they were taking the test and getting certificates when a couple of NCOs rushed in and pulled the instructor outside.

"They talked to the instructor for a minute and then he came in and they told us what had happened," said Pruitt. "It felt like my heart just got ripped out of my chest. It was the hardest thing that I've ever had to endure. Hearing the words that not only Devin but Sgt. Bell, Spec. Voakes and Sgt. Powell, all four of them and a civilian. They were all gone. To hear something like that, it's an unexplainable feeling. You don't know what to think, you get put in a total state of shock."

He and the other drivers had to stay there while they figured out when they could get a chopper to fly them back to Mihtarlam. Then they found out that the bodies of the deceased would be taken to Jalalabad, where they were. It was the first step of the journey back to Bagram and then to Dover. They asked if they could pay their last respects.

"So when the time came, they gave us a few minutes and we were able to walk in the room where they were holding them all."

Some of the other soldiers were preparing to perform the ceremonial loading of the transfer cases onto the plane and Pruitt and the others asked if they could do it.

"We were there. It should only be fitting that we as their brothers and sister, we perform the ceremony. They gave us the okay so I was fortunate enough to be one of the ones that was able to carry my friends to put them on the flight to send them back to their families, which was, by far to date, one of the most horrible things I have ever done in my life," said Pruitt. "But being able to do that and give them that final salute was an honor and a privilege."

"The final roll call," he added, "is when the first sergeant stands up and he calls a few soldiers out that are there and then when he gets to the soldiers that have passed they do three final roll calls. They start out with their rank and their last name, then their rank and their last name and first name. Then their rank, last name, middle name and first name. That's the final roll call. That's when it really starts to set in, at least for me, when you hear them call their name for the last time."

The recommendations by soldiers in the reports offer some insight into what went wrong that day. Soldiers suggested ANP checkpoints and better armored vehicles. One soldier noted what came to be a common theme: "the convoy commander has the power to make decisions on movement and if he decided to be complacent it puts the soldiers at a greater risk, I believe."

Another soldier said "our patrols need to be more deliberate with our movement, clearing anything that could possibly be an IED."

"When coming upon suspected IED emplacement locations, units should dismount and conduct a recon and clear the area out to 200 meters," said another soldier.

"I feel that dropping dismounts before crossing into known IED hotspots and varying their distance from each other and sending them approximately 150 meters in the 3 and 9 o'clock of the route will enable the dismounts to either find or get the insurgents away from the firing point," said a soldier from EOD.

Enlow wishes they had better equipment, like the new Oshkosh MRAPs that were due to be delivered, or the new MaxxPros that were being held up. They were all higher off the ground, with v-shaped hulls.

"Previous battle damage combined with difficulty in receiving parts," reported one soldier, meant that one of the bigger vehicles that they had was out of circulation. The biggest, the RG31, though the most armored, was kept from the lead in the convoy because it can fit a litter in it, in case of an injury.

"The reason we don't want him up front is they're less maneuverable," said Enlow. "More blind spots. They can take a hit better but it's harder to maneuver things and they get stuck and have to go slower through it."

Enlow, running it over in his mind again, regrets the vehicle assignments.

"If I had a different list of people, there might have been fewer people. If I had a different vehicle up front, there might have been fewer casualties."

Adding insult to injury, immediately afterward "there was a knee-jerk reaction from the task force commander that no MATVs will be the lead vehicle."

In an obscure comment section of one of the sworn statements, one soldier captured perhaps what all understood, but that went unsaid in all the other testimonies:

"No matter what you do, the enemy gets a vote."

Chapter 12: Sandstorm

Though the wave of grief went ever outward, at the center of it the soldiers in Devin's platoon had to bear their grief, or subdue it, in order to keep focused. They were only two months into a yearlong deployment.

"I think three days afterward we had our next mission," remembered Enlow. "Right in the same area. Right up Alingar Valley to do our job. All we could do was affect the things inside our sphere of influence. So I said 'Let's take our rage, our betrayal, our sadness and focus it on our mission.'"

Not long after, a two-star general in charge of Northern Afghanistan started an inquiry about the IED attack and found that the 164th MP Company was spread out over six different bases. In July, new orders came and the mission changed. In order to bring the 164th together, they assigned them to a Joint Combat Operations Post (JCOP) called Puli Saiad. About nine kilometers outside of Bagram Airfield, their mission was to do patrols with the Afghan National Army in order to keep Bagram safe. Their base was located near a bridge over the Pamaher River, a tributary of the Kabul River. The road was one of the main access roads to Bagram.

"Some pencil-pusher decided we had experienced too many losses and pulled the entire unit to Parwan province, which is around Bagram," remembered Enlow. "So we could go pull air security duty for Bagram, which we felt like was a betrayal because we were invested. That mission [cost] the lives of our comrades and to be pulled from that we felt that would break the commitment. If we can just turn around and shut it down because we're not needed then why the fuck are we out there to begin with?"

Pruitt admits that he was pleased with the move. They were able to start over. Maybe it would be different.

"Mihtarlam was just a bad area and it was such a hard time to figure out who was doing it. We could never catch them," he said. "It was to the point where your worry was twice as bad, having to go back to that same area at least two to three times a week."

Misgivings aside, the new mission was still a vital part of the war. Some members of the platoon went on missions with US

Special Forces. Others maintained security around Bagram, the central airfield of the war.

Their primary focus was "to patrol and deter enemy actions against the base," said Johnson, describing their new mission.

"If something happened we got sent to where it came from," he continued. "Whenever Bagram would get intel that there was a cache or a high-value target somewhere in our area they would send our unit to go get them."

On one of his last missions in Afghanistan, Johnson's squad found and arrested someone who had launched rockets toward Bagram.

"That guy turned around and told where weapons caches were, gave out locations of safe-houses, gave a roster of the Taliban members in that area and locations of them," said Johnson.

"That was in Puli Saiad," remembered Pruitt. "We were basically the outer security for Bagram Air Field. We would go out and we would do daily and nightly patrols driving around the outside perimeter of the base. I want to say we did a fifty-mile radius outside of the base, trying to deter any activity. If there were rumors that there was somebody who was known to try and place IEDs we would try to capture them."

On October 7, 2011, after ten years of war, peace talks began with the Taliban.

At one point during their time at Puli Saiad, Stacey Jordan remembers one of the four-wheel drive trucks getting stuck in what they called "moon dust."

"It's a really fine sand," she said.

For the soldiers, it was another reminder that the land was hostile to them. Things could still go wrong. Their feeling of relative safety, like the shifting of sands, was impermanent.

At another point, an IED explosion destroyed half of the main road leading to their base. There was only one lane that was usable; only one truck at a time could fit through.

Another bottleneck.

"We had to go make sure they didn't plant another one every day," said Stacey.

On the rides out to make the checks, they would often encounter shepherds and large flocks of sheep. Sheep apparently had universal right of way in that area, because the shepherds would drive the sheep across the main highway at any and all times.

A few of the soldiers had been going on two-week R&R leave. When Josh Pruitt returned from his, it was back to daily missions. He was a driver in their convoys.

"It was the main road in and out of the little village that our JCOP was on and they had already, a few weeks prior, had hit somebody else's vehicle and blew out half of the road so there was only about half the road left and it was just wide enough to get our vehicles through. We had spent weeks and weeks and weeks stopping at that point to make sure it was okay. So one night we did our stop, we did our check, everything was okay and then we hopped in the trucks and started driving. I was in the second vehicle through. I drove up to it and I remember my team leader at that point in time telling me I had a little bit of extra room to the right because there was a ditch to the right. I had a few more inches to go so I turned a little bit more to get more room so I didn't fall in the hole and they hit the button."

The blast was early by about two seconds.

"Imagine a roman candle going off right underneath you," said Pruitt, explaining the intensity of the detonation. "Multiply that, I would say, by about a hundred. It is loud, it disorientates you. It sends a concussion feeling in your chest so hard it feels like somebody took a basketball and shot it out of a fast pitch machine and hit you in the chest. To me that's how it felt. It's something that sticks with you forever."

The explosion knocked him out for a second, blew out the other half of the road, leaving the ruined truck and its passed out driver in a crater-like hole.

"I woke up and I was looking at concrete-covered windshield," said Pruitt. "I remember looking for my legs. I knew what had happened once I opened up my eyes but your first reaction is to check and make sure you're okay and then check if everybody else was okay and thankfully everybody was okay at that time."

161

It was virtually the same scenario as Mihtarlam, and even though they performed the dismounted checks, they were still vulnerable to an IED. This time, however, they had better trucks. These had the v-hull. On this occasion, the better equipment saved them.

"My ears rang for a couple days," said Pruitt. "Even though I had the ear protection and stuff like that on. Had a little bit of a foggy memory. I got lucky."

The truck was so damaged that they had to call for help to get it out of the hole and onto a flat bed.

"The back tires were six feet off of the ground," said Pruitt. "It had to be lifted out."

In March of 2012, after outrage at Afghan civilian casualties, the Taliban canceled peace talks. Hostility toward American troops spiked. President Hamid Karzai issued an order that all troops under NATO command should stay on their bases.

Powerful sandstorms came through at times, covering everything with dust. They stayed on base during those storms.

"We got through the rest of the year," said Enlow. "We had some soldiers come and go from our organic unit. They came in, couldn't hack it or thought we were crazy, whatever the case may be, and got moved somewhere else."

For some, their deployment strengthened them. They learned what they could handle. They found their limits.

Others were just waiting for the deployment, like a sandstorm, to blow over.

Chapter 13: Shockwave

By the time the news of Devin's death hit the small towns of Wayland and Cohocton, the wave of grief had become a hurricane-strength storm surge. Schoolmates, school employees, anyone who had heard of Devin's service and her accomplishments in sports, her friends, family, friends of friends, and friends of family. The whole area shook heads in disbelief and shared the Snyders' mourning. She was a loved one to many more people than she knew.

"The day they came to our door was the worst day of our lives," remembered Ed.

President Obama, having just given a speech celebrating his economic policy the day before at a Chrysler plant in Toledo, Ohio, played golf that Saturday.[63] It was an ordinary day for most. On Monday, he held his monthly meeting about Afghanistan and Pakistan with his national security advisors. He was briefed on "progress in implementing our strategy for Pakistan and Afghanistan following the death of Osama bin Laden" as well as the "progress being made to build and sustain the Afghan National Security Forces."[64] It is likely that they spoke of the recent losses, despite a focus on the progress.

Natasha was driving down the road in Virginia when her dad called. She was worried at first but when she answered, he didn't say anything so she hung up thinking he pocket-dialed her or something. He called her back immediately.

The only words that he could get out were "Devin is dead."

Natasha pulled over. She was shaking.

"What are you talking about? This isn't true," she said. "I just talked to her this morning."

"This is a joke. You're lying," she said.

"Natasha, this is real," said Ed. "They were standing at the doorway and they said she was killed."

She told him that she would be home as soon as possible. A friend who was in the car with her took over driving while Natasha called her command.

"They put me on leave and I was on the flight home the next day," she said.

Danette and Greg McInnis were out driving on the warm June day, heading down the hill on a curvy state road to the next town for ice cream.

Dineen was calling. They put her on speakerphone.

"Hello?" answered Danette. There was a pause. She immediately knew something was wrong.

"Two men were just here to tell us that Devin was killed," said Dineen.

They told her they would be right over and they turned the car around.

On the ride home, they called their oldest son, Reese, who was a senior in high school, and told him to take his friend home and come to Aunt Dineen's house.

The car ride was full of skepticism and terror.

"I didn't believe a thing that she said. I was like 'No'," said Greg. "It's somebody else. Something is screwed up."

"I couldn't even breathe," remembered Danette.

Her mother was already there with Dineen and Ed when Danette arrived.

After some time privately grieving, Greg took a call from Jeff Englert. They had both been coaches for the school, and they were friends. Jeff was in New Jersey with his son at a scouting event for quarterbacks. He had received a phone call from his wife, giving him the news. Still in disbelief, he called up Greg McInnis.

"Greg, I'm just calling to get things straight. I heard that something might have happened to Devin?"

"She's gone, Jeff."

"How did you find out?"

Someone had already posted it on Facebook. His wife had received a text about it.

"Are you shitting me?" said Greg. Their daughter Kayden was spending the night with a friend and they were worried that she might hear before they had a chance to tell her in person. Luckily, she was outside camping and had no access to social media.

164

"We got to her in the morning," remembered Danette. "We got her in the car and got going down the road a ways and after a bit we told her that we have bad news and we told her that Devin had been killed."

She was just turning eleven.

"Our kids were great," said Greg, reflecting on how they handled the news. "It was hard but they were pretty tough."

"They were tough, but they were upset," added Danette.

"They were solemn and caring and did whatever you needed," said Greg.

Alyssa Englert had finished the spring semester at the University of Hartford and was home for summer break. She was in Rochester at the time.

"I was actually at a Redwings game with a couple of friends and one of the friends that I was with either got a call from someone or a text," said Alyssa.

Her first reaction was "What do you mean? She's just gone?"

They watched the fireworks at the end of the game and drove home.

"I get home and just go to bed," said Alyssa. "It's not happening. It's not real."

But in the morning, a flood of texts came. Facebook was filling up with tribute posts.

"I had finally come to terms and realized what had happened," she said.

More friends started reading about Devin's death on Facebook. People were posting tributes. Statuses came up reading "RIP Devin Snyder."

Emily May saw a post like that while at her friend Dan Reynolds' house.

"At first it was like, that can't be true," she said. "We waited and waited and wanted to text Dineen but we knew we couldn't be bugging her…We saw more and more things coming up and then it was on the news. That night was the first shock. Dan was very close with her too. He broke down. I broke down. We talked until I don't even know what time in the morning."

Mikayla Sick received a call from her sister, Ally, who had also been on the track team with Devin.

"Did you hear the news?"

"No."

"Devin was killed in Afghanistan."

"Shut up, Ally. You don't say that kind of thing."

"I'm sorry Kay but it's real. It's real."

"What do you mean?"

"I'm sorry. I'm sorry."

She checked Facebook, and people were posting all over her wall.

The shock spread.

Meaghan Oas was out that Saturday night at a bar by nearby Loon Lake. She kept getting calls from a friend who was related to the Snyders. She ignored her call until she received a text: "You need to call me."

Oas stepped outside for a moment and called her.

"Devin was killed."

"Shut up! No she wasn't!"

"No, she was."

"I didn't want to believe it," recalled Oas. "I hung up the phone and just stood there and tears rolled down my face. I just start crying. I went back inside to say I have to go and I couldn't stop crying."

She went back to a friend's house and began calling people, sending texts, and scouring social media for any information about what happened.

"At that point I'm on my phone trying to figure out if it's true...You don't want to believe it," she said, but by the next day, she knew it was real.

It was later that night when Dave Saxton heard.

"I think I had gone to a party and I drove home. I was in my driveway and I got a phone call from Bailey Hill, another track teammate of Devin's. I thought it was just like 'I'm drunk somewhere, come pick me up.' I answered the phone and she was just like...whimpering."

"Are you okay? What's going on?"

"I just found out that Devin was killed."

"What are you talking about?"

"Did you hear about this? Do you know about it? What do you know about it?" said Bailey in a state of panic.

"Where did you hear it from?"

She had heard from someone who had talked to Dineen.

"Is it true?" asked Bailey.

"I have no idea. I'll try to find out."

There wasn't much for him to do. He knew that if the family was told, then it was true. But he also knew that Bailey called him hoping to hear that it was a mistake.

"I'll find out, I'll find out," he said. But they both knew that they had already heard the truth.

"It's a small town," said former Supervisor Jack Zigenfus. "Small towns have advantages and disadvantages. Disadvantage is that everybody knows everybody's business. So when you have something like what happened to Devin, everybody knows."

"My son Nick had called me and told me," said Judge Ron Snyder. "He was crying. He wasn't close to her but he knew her and he was her cousin. It was devastating. Even to this day it's tough to talk about. It still hurts. Even though I wasn't all that close. She was just one of those super girls."

The day after Devin was killed, Coach Julie Martin received a phone call. Her brother had been at his hunting camp with a group of guys, one of whom was Greg McInnis. McInnis had heard about her death the night that it happened and mentioned it to the group. When Martin heard the news, she went out on her front porch to be alone. She sat there, in shock, for a long time. How could she be gone? She was so young and full of life.

"Living in such a small community, everyone knows everyone," said Martin. She didn't expect that anything would happen to Devin, and even when Zach Smith from Hornell died, she assumed that would be as close as the war would get to their little town.

Martin went to see Ed and Dineen on June 5th, the day after Devin died. She gave them each a hug and told them that she would be there for them. There was little else that could be said. Family had already gathered there, and were sitting in various rooms of the house. There was a lot of support.

For the first few days, Martin was still struck with disbelief.

"It was the sort of thing that happens to other people. It doesn't happen in a small town."

"I think it broke everybody's heart," remembered Mikayla Sick. "It just became so real. It affected everybody around us. Everybody in this state, really."

Mikayla went to visit the family after a couple of days. Her bright blue eyes and blonde hair, to the Snyders, were a reminder of Devin.

"I'll never forget it," she said. "Her brother gave me a hug and he wouldn't let go of me and he kept telling me 'You have her eyes. You know that? You have her eyes.' I was speechless. To me, it was like, she lives in me now. I couldn't really let it soak in yet. I think he was just so in shock still."

But after the shock wore off, she saw Ed a few times.

"He just breaks down," she said.

He would see her in town somewhere, and at first he glance, he sees Devin. Then he realizes that it's Mikayla, and a kind of disappointment sets in.

"He cries every time he sees me and it's hard. I'm not her. I'm sorry I'm not."

The shockwave of grief continued traveling ever outward, all the way to Alaska, where the 164th MP Company was stationed. Those on rear deployment, like Jessica Jeffords, took the loss to their company very hard. She had just been home in Colorado and flew back to Alaska, arriving late at night. She woke up early for morning PT, took a shower, and was in her room. The music video for

"Collide," a new song by Kid Rock and Sheryl Crow, was playing on TV.

"I got a phone call from Dineen," remembered Jessica. "She was crying and I couldn't understand anything she said and the first thing that popped into my head was they got into a fight.

She had previously spoke with Dineen to let her know that she was going to surprise Devin and come to New York in July when she would be home on leave. But Dineen kept crying and Jessica still couldn't really understand her.

"You know people get in fights all of the time," said Jessica, trying to reassure her. "We always work through fights. We'll work through everything."

"And I just kept talking and talking and talking," remembered Jessica. It was about four minutes of talking before she stopped short at the word *dead.*

"What did you just say?" asked Jessica, incredulous.

On the other line, Dineen was crying so hard that she could barely breathe.

"Devin's dead. Devin's dead. She's gone. She's gone. She's dead."

"My heart sunk into my stomach and I thought I was going to throw up," said Jessica.

Despite the Army's strict regulations against it, Jessica walked straight out of her room in her bathrobe. People were telling her to get dressed, but she walked silently by them. She still had the phone to her ear. The same people were now following her, yelling at her to go back and get dressed. She couldn't hear Dineen over the yells, so Dineen said she would call her back later. With people still following her, she finally made her way to a friend's room, who had picked her up some cigarettes. She knocked.

He opened the door.

"What the fuck? Get dressed!" he said. "Hurry up before you get in trouble."

"Give me the cigarettes right now," she said.

Unsure what was going on, he gave her the cigarettes. She grabbed a lighter from his room and went out to her car and locked herself inside, still wearing just a robe.

"I didn't care what the fuck kind of trouble I was going to get into. When everyone was at work I didn't show up to work. I knew I was going to be in a shit ton of trouble. I sat in my car and just chain-smoked, I called Smith and said 'I need more cigarettes and I want beer.' He brought me both. I had to put my keys outside because its a DUI if I had my keys inside my car. So I was drinking inside my car. Smoking my cigarettes and just watching my phone blow up."

Most of the calls were from people in her company, or wives of the company, trying to confirm if the rumor was true. Overwhelmed, she decided not to talk to anyone.

All of a sudden her First Sergeant appeared and he knocked on her window.

"Can you come out?"

"Nope."

"I'll make you a deal," he said. "You can sit in here but can you go inside and get dressed?"

So she went inside and got dressed, but she came back out and to her surprise, the First Sergeant had brought her more beer and cigarettes.

"Call me when you want to talk," he said. "I'm taking your keys."

Meanwhile, Dineen and Ed travelled to the mortuary at Dover Air Force Base in Delaware.

"I guess this is the way it normally works when someone is killed in the service," said Jack Zigenfus. "They go to Dover and it takes a while just to get the person back. It was very, very difficult on Dineen and Ed."

"It was so dragged out it just kept the hurt going because it took so long to get the body over here and get the arrangements going," said Judge Snyder.

In Alaska, Jessica was still having trouble dealing with it.

"The only people I wanted to talk to was my family but my family was out of the country so I had no one to talk to, no one to lean on. No support whatsoever, so I was depressed."

Trying to figure out how to deal with it, she went to her First Sergeant to talk.

"Can I go to her funeral? I want to go to her funeral," she asked.

"No, you're not allowed to. You don't have leave."

"I have leave. I have like 28 days of leave. I have plenty of leave."

"No, you just got back from leave."

Her command was not going to let her go.

"So I basically went on a drunk bender," she said. "Just kind of drank myself to sleep. Then one morning Sergeant Major Orvis called me."

"I just wanted to see how you were doing," he said. "I know you guys were like two peas in a pod."

They talked for hours. She talked mostly and he listened.

"He was my only support," she said.

Then she told him how they wouldn't let her go to her funeral.

"No, you'll go. I'm going to see what I can do."

The next day Jessica became her special escort. She had to attend classes that dictated how to behave. She flew to Philadelphia and then was taken to Dover. There were many other escorts, but Jessica was a "special escort," that is, she knew Devin. There were different trainings to be done, and she was isolated from the others. The Snyders had already returned home.

"I was put in a different hotel than everyone," she remembered. "It was like a week and a half I was in this freaking hotel room by myself. All I was doing was drinking and smoking."

When they brought her back to Dover for more training, she was determined to find Devin and see her. She found her way into one of the morgue areas in the back. There were many flag-draped coffins. All were labeled by numbers, not by names.

Terrified of opening the wrong casket, Jessica was shaking and crying. She sat down.

Fortunately a kind-hearted Sergeant First Class came in and found her. He sat down by her.

"You know you can't be back here," he said.

"I know," she said, crying.

"You want to see her?"

"Yeah, I do."

He took her to see Devin.

"In a way I wish I didn't, but in a way I wouldn't have believed it. I had to identify her body anyways and make sure she was presentable for her family. But I was all by myself. It was the most depressing time of my life."

Chapter 14: A Somber Homecoming

As the people of Cohocton waited for Devin's remains to return, the village took on a somber feeling. Flags and yellow ribbons tied to trees and telephone poles all the along the main streets waved in the breezes, but only half-heartedly, as if the wind was nothing more than a sigh.

Plexiglas letters on the sign outside of the fire hall read "We Remember. Army Specialist Devin Snyder." A sign outside of the church read "Thoughts and prayers to the Snyder family." In the window of a store, "Forever in our hearts."

"I remember my parents were both very upset about it," recalled David Saxton. "I think because of what she was to the community and my mom worked with her mom and how much of a nice girl she was, but also they were scared. They were terrified. If it can happen to a cute, blonde girl from your high school, you best believe it can happen to a dude who is probably not signing up for the easiest job in the army."

Despite their fears, the Saxtons and David went to Rochester. He found that it gave him some perspective on being an officer, and the decisions that have to be made as a leader.

"I needed to see that because I need to experience every single thing that happens, because that's always going to be in the back of my mind for every decision making process for whatever I do," he said. "Also, you need to be there, you need to be present, you need to be seen, as someone who is in the military and as someone who is showing their support."

So David put on his cadet uniform and wore it, maybe for the first time, with pride. He worried how it would look. Would people in the community think he was trying to take attention away from honoring Devin? Would his enlisted friends tease him for being a cadet? Would veterans think that he had taken the "easy way" because he was in officer school? Was he doing the right thing?

"I'm glad that I did it but I was scared out of my mind," he said.

The family rode in a chartered bus from Cohocton to Rochester following the Genesee River Valley north along the interstate. Dineen and Ed sat in one front seat. Danette and Greg sat in the other.

Greg was thinking about the route they would take. They had already met with various people throughout the week and had planned out the ride. He looked over at Ed and he looked numb.

At the airport, they were on the tarmac as Devin's casket was taken off the plane.

"Everything was in slow motion," said Greg. "Even the plane taxiing was half speed of normal taxiing. The whole thing was in slow motion."

Jessica was there, escorting Devin's remains. There was a ceremony and bagpipers played. They boarded the bus and the procession left the airport and followed a route home that was partly on the highway and partly through the small towns.

The casket was escorted by a mile-long motorcade made up of police vehicles, the white hearse, a tour bus, and a hundred and fifty motorcycle riders from the group the Patriot Guard Riders. This non-profit, volunteer group seeks to "shield the mourning family and their friends from interruptions" created by protest groups, such as the Westboro Baptist Church, and to show "respect for our fallen heroes, their families, and their communities."

At the front of the motorcade was Chris Smith of Hornell, State Trooper and father of Lance Corporal Zach Smith, the nineteen year old Marine who died in Afghanistan in January 2010.

At every overpass, community members, Veterans of Foreign Wars, and The American Legion were there welcoming them with flags signs and salutes. Cars pulled over out of respect.

The sky was overcast and the wind was blowing. Birds chirped in the trees above the onlookers.

Danette saw an old man who looked like he might have difficulty walking, sitting along the side of the road in his Army uniform. As they passed, he stood up and saluted them.

The towns were packed with people.

"Every town you went through, schools were out," remembered former Mayor Tom Cox. "Flags. While that bus was coming back you could have heard a pin drop. There was not a sound. It was like going through a ghost town even though thousands of people lined that road from Rochester to Cohocton. It was something you never want to go through again but like I say, you didn't think it was going to happen in your town. It was on TV but it doesn't come to you. But it does, so we found out."

"That was honestly one of the most beautiful things I have ever seen in my entire life," said David Saxton. "Thousands of people. I was expecting that some would stop their day. Some fire departments would come out. Some VFWs. Some at the Legion would come outside. I didn't expect thousands of people. I remember going around the corner in Rush. I'll never forget this. Going around the corner in Rush, there was some lady there who was just crying. I just remember thinking that lady has no idea who this girl is."

"And then we went through Lima and the whole Christian school was outside," remembered Danette, "and they were ringing the bell. It was like that all the way down through."

The procession rode through the bus loop of Wayland-Cohocton Central School, past hundreds of students and teachers who lined the street. They were holding flags taken off the walls of their classrooms, women and girls were crying, boys who could not sit still for long in a classroom stood statue-still, mesmerized by the endless stream of passing cars and motorcycles.

"Those kids just stood there so respectfully," said Danette. "I'm sure that's something some of them will remember forever. We were just very blessed at the outpouring of people we had."

One group of girls from the track team held a white bed sheet spray-painted with a red heart and the words "Welcome Home, Sgt. Devin Twiggy Snyder."

In Cohocton, the Elementary School emptied its classrooms and community members lined the streets as well. The elderly sat in chairs. Babies sat in strollers. Anyone who could hold one, held a flag. Handwritten or hand-painted signs read, "We will miss you" and "Thank you."

Fire trucks sat on either side of the road, ladders extended toward the center, an American flag draped between them. The

175

white hearse passed beneath on the way through town. It stopped at the funeral home upon returning to Wayland. The family, at that time, was allowed to see Devin's remains before the calling hours.

"I will never forget the cries that came out of my mom," said Natasha. "That's just a noise I'm never going to forget. I'll never forget seeing my dad break down and cry because he is just such a strong person and I had never seen him cry. When we actually got to see Devin I will never forget the reaction of my little brother. All of that just killed me."

Alyssa Englert was also on the bus with the family. Since that experience, Alyssa admits that she has not been the same.

However, her own strength was a comfort to the family that day. The burden that they had to carry and that they still carry was made lighter by Alyssa's presence. Unfortunately, Alyssa still has to carry that weight with her. It has made her more humble, she says, more reserved, maybe even more of a wallflower. She feels the pain of Devin's death every time she visits Dineen at school or sees Damien or other members of the family. The healing that is supposed to take place over time has not really happened.

"I think a part of me just has not been able to come back since that day and since that month of events that happened afterward," she said. "I kind of lost a bit of myself when I had to go through that. I can't imagine what Dineen and Ed, their whole family, feel. I still don't think they're fully recovered, I'm not sure if they ever will be. Or if I ever will be. Or if you can from something like that."

Chapter 15: Catharsis

The community knew that many people would want to come to the funeral to show their support, so it was decided that the memorial service should be held at the Cohocton Sports Complex, where so many of Devin's soccer games had taken place. The community wanted to make it special and, to whatever extent they could, to take the burden off Ed and Dineen. If there was one thing that Cohoctonites knew, it was how to handle large crowds in the middle of the village. An all-volunteer operation still ran the Sports Complex, including numerous games and tournaments, and community volunteers ran the Fall Foliage Festival. Some were the same people. The infrastructure was in place and the people knew how to work together.

"Every night we were here in this room," said former Mayor Cox, indicating the space inside one of the old buildings in town, called the Cohocton Development Corporation. He was one of a group of volunteers helping to plan the day. The funeral director, Chip Baird, had years of experience, but little with the protocol of military funerals. Cox knew the protocol, and worked with Baird to plan it out.

"He came down and we went through how they were going to enter the complex and the route they were going to take... How to set up the memorial area, where the band was going to sit, where the family was going to sit, where the parking was going to be," said Cox. "It was a lot of coordination to do in about four days, but we worked with the volunteers."

Greg McInnis attended the meetings to be sure that everything was done according to the family's wishes. He had another idea and was working on it outside of the meetings.

Over fifty local organizations, most outside of Cohocton, offered help or financial support. People in town cleaned off their porches and trimmed their front yards. American flags were out everywhere.

Matt Bondgren, Cohocton resident and soccer coach, was one of the volunteers on the grounds of the Sports Complex.

"We worked at the complex and there were just scads of people," he remembered. "Planting flowerbeds, weed-whacking, mowing. I remember all the people still walking around in a state of shock. My daughter is three and she's trying to figure out what's going on, and my sons. We're trying to explain it to them, because they're all with us doing all these things, and I'll never forget the feeling of complete sadness."

"This goes back to why I love my community so much," said Emily May. "Everybody came together. Even if nobody knew who she was before, they cared and they prayed. They felt bad and they did whatever they could to help Dineen and Ed and anybody else who was close to her."

They had been expecting glitches.

One was that the Westboro Baptist Church was rumored to be scouting the area, planning a protest at Devin's funeral. Famous for demonstrating at the funerals of fallen soldiers, the Westboro Baptist Church believes that our country is experiencing the wrath of God because we permit homosexuality.[65] They claim that the "modern militant homosexual movement [poses] a clear and present danger to the survival of America, exposing our nation to the wrath of God as in 1898 B.C. at Sodom and Gomorrah."

They believe that they are the prophets of God.

"God has sent us, His people, to deliver His words," reads a response to one of the Frequently Asked Questions on their website. "Every time you ratchet up your sin and rebellion, in direct response to our words, God punishes you again. That means God is confirming the words of His servants."

Some of the local radio stations started picking up the story. Mayor Cox, frustrated that the media was emphasizing and sensationalizing the protest while glossing over Devin's death, began calling some of the shows. He told them that they had, that week, passed local ordinances to limit any public protest to certain areas in the village, areas out of sight of the sports complex. The police chief had security set up to block any protesters who might show up and the motorcycle group, The Patriot Guard Riders, came to form a wall of bikes to shield the bereaved from any picket signs or shouting.

It turned out to be all for nothing, as the WBC never did show up.

"They are fortunate that they didn't come here," said Greg. "I know what would have happened. I grew up with these guys."

"There's a big farm family and their oldest sister lives next to Dineen," explained Danette. "They were very close to Devin too."

"They would have gotten beaten up bad," said Greg.

At some point during that time, Devin was promoted to Sergeant posthumously. Her paperwork was being processed at the time of her death, but it was fast-tracked by the Army as a way of honoring a fallen comrade.

When the day of the memorial service came, it was very hot, but periodically there was a strong breeze. As if the winds, too, were weeping, they were gusting to 16 mph, alternating with periods of stillness. It changed direction many times that day, from SE to NW and back. People began arriving around nine-thirty in the morning and, about twenty minutes later, the whole complex was full. The chairs on the field were full, the bleachers were full, and people were standing. The crowd was settling in. Over the gates, again held by two fire truck ladders, was a giant American flag. The ceremony was about to begin, and it was quiet. The wind, which had been still for a while, rose suddenly, pulling all of the American flags taut all at once, as if to signal the beginning of the service. The gust continued blowing, and the only sound was of flags flapping in the wind.

"They all were flapping in unison and I don't even know how to describe it," said Danette.

"Those flags were all whipping at attention and snapping," said Greg. "It's like it blew through and then it stopped. It was eerie. If you're spiritual, and I'm not, something was working. Something was working at that time. It really was."

As the service began, bagpipes played "Amazing Grace" as the flag-covered casket was hauled on a black caisson by two black horses. The caisson driver steered them around the school's Sports Complex, past a line of saluting veterans, closely followed by two Reverends in white robes. Behind them, troops in olive drab uniforms marched in step, gold buttons shining in the sun.

The caisson had been Greg's mission. He had looked for an appropriate carriage to carry the casket, but couldn't find one that was as dignified as he wanted it to be. Finally he found a man out of the Philadelphia area that sometimes worked at Arlington. He had a caisson and could bring his horses in a trailer, so Greg hired him. The effect was that the ceremony had the air of a Kennedy funeral. For Cohocton, it was just as devastating a loss.

Community members sat in the spectator stands just across from the fields where they had watched Devin in the Spud Jug game. For close friends and family, white folding chairs lined the fields, the kind often found at weddings, another thing Devin would never see. There, the girls' soccer team sat together wearing the uniform of their time with her: their jerseys.

They bought a wreath and walked it to the casket and placed it on a wreath stand. Gene Miller, the owner of Punky Hollow, sat with Julie Martin.

"As sad a day as it was, it was one of the most beautiful services that I've ever seen," she said.

The wind was gusty all day, but during one of the lulls, a bald eagle circled over the complex and then soared away. Though recently recovered to some degree, the bald eagle had to be reintroduced to the Finger Lakes after the DDT epidemic wiped out the population during the seventies. To see one was still rare, and for it to appear over the village, especially directly over the ceremony, was very unlikely. Some took it as a sign that Devin was still with them, or that Devin's spirit was blessed, or that perhaps something greater also mourned her loss.

"That was a hard day," said Emily May. "There were so many people that cared. People were crying, but people were laughing thinking about her memory. It was just such a whirlwind of different emotions for people. We just wanted to welcome her home one last time I guess. And to thank her for everything that she has done."

Dressed in his Army uniform, David Saxton fought to maintain his decorum. He would not break down at the event, but the experience did make him reflect again on his own military service. He was inspired to be a better soldier, to be a better leader.

The event also evoked some fears that are no doubt common to young soldiers.

"The scariest thing ... was when they gave the flag to her mom," he remembered. "That was terrifying. Yes, that is my friend, the friend of my mom, but you're crazy if you don't see, I'm the flag and that's my mom."

"It was great but I wish we were there for a different celebration," admitted Mikayla Sick. "A promotion or something. I wish we were all there celebrating her successes. It was just sad."

"I probably hadn't cried that much in years," said Judge Snyder.

Benedictions and Bible passages focused on the promises of the afterlife, including Isaiah 25:6, which reads, "On this mountain the Lord of hosts will make for all peoples a feast of fat things, a feast of wine on the lees, of fat things full of marrow, of wine on the lees well refined."

But the mourners were perhaps not yet ready for the consolation prize that is eternal life, and many tears were yet to be shed.

Then attendees walked about a half-mile in a long funeral procession, to the churchyard where Devin would be buried. The caisson carried her on the final leg of her journey.

"There wasn't a peep from anybody the entire time," remembered Mikayla Sick. As she walked and cried, the police chief held her hand. "It was the quietest parade you had ever seen."

Zion Lutheran Church is hidden behind a farm, across from a hayfield where in early summer the round green-tinted bales of fresh-cut hay stand in a herd like the animals they will soon feed. The small, white church with a tall bell tower is at the end of a dead end road. A large pine tree almost covers the steeple. There are two crosses at the entryway and many graves from the late 1800s, when the valley was being settled. There are also many veterans of all of the wars there, including other Snyders.

The gravesite is very near the highway, probably fifty yards. The cemetery is no larger than a soccer field, but many of the names are familiar ones to those who live in the area. The large letters sprawl across the stones like names on the backs of jerseys.

Surrounding the graveyard is a highway ramp and raised access road that form a sort of natural amphitheater. The Patriot Guard Riders lined the road above the graveyard, forming a wall of flags. Friends, family, and community members followed the procession below to Zion Lutheran Church, filling the bottom of the earthen bowl.

She was buried at the back of the cemetery, marked by a red-pink granite stone, next to which is planted a red Norway maple tree. The inscription is the Serenity Prayer, a favorite of Devin's:

"God, grant me the serenity to accept the things I cannot change, the courage to change the things I can, and the wisdom to know the difference."

After the funeral, Cohocton was a changed place. For one, the war in Afghanistan was no longer a far-off, abstract war. It had come home.

"I think it made people look deeper into what's going on around them," said David Saxton, of Devin's death. "I think if it did anything, it broke people out of their bubble."

"You hear on the news all the time about soldiers dying," said Meaghan Oas. "This happened, that happened, five were killed. You hear all of that but when it's somebody from your hometown it's different. Whether you knew her or you didn't know her, it's still going to affect you. I would hope that it would affect you."

That effect, for a time anyway, may have been healing. For a town still divided over decade-old issues, such as the school merger and the wind turbines, the funeral brought people together, repaired some of those divides, and perhaps helped the community remember their better selves.

"I think that the community just came together and still is coming together in her memory," said May. "It will always be a tragedy."

"To see a community as small as Cohocton pull together the way they did and show their support at that event was amazing," said Coach Julie Martin. "It was like nothing I have ever seen and probably something I will never see again in my life."

182

"Kids will complain that it is boring growing up in a small town," said Martin. "But it has its advantages too. It is good to know that people will still come together and be there for you, if you need it, to help you get through the tough times."

Meaghan Oas echoed her sentiment.

"Growing up I hated living in a small town," said Oas. "If something happens to you, give it less than twenty-four hours and everybody is going to know. I hated everyone knowing everything about everyone. But after Devin had passed away, seeing all these little communities come together, that's what it's all about."

"Everybody put aside their differences in support of the same cause," said Mikayla Sick, "and I think that changed a lot of people. I think there are fewer enemies from all that."

Later, a luminary, or candlelight ceremony, was also organized. The grieving hands of those sitting in the stands at dusk held hundreds of candles. Those in attendance purchased candles in white bags on the field, lighting up the grounds. A scholarship in honor of Devin is awarded each year from those funds.

In Alaska, the Army held a memorial service also. A giant American flag served as the backdrop for the stage. Four helmets atop of four rifles stood over eight boots at the center of the stage.

The General spoke.

"Devin Snyder. She had a smile that lit up a room. She was a constant team player… and an excellent soldier."

"These soldiers contributed to the success of the 164th Military Police Company through their unique abilities and attributes, and while none of these soldiers can be replaced, the 164th MP Company is still dedicated to completing its mission in Afghanistan…They will continue to fight to honor Joshua, Chris, Devin, and Robert because that's what these great soldiers would have wanted…Ralph Waldo Emerson once said, 'Our chief want is someone who will inspire us to be what we know we could be.' These four soldiers inspired not only their families, but all of us. These heroes will never be forgotten."

Then friends of Powell and Bell gave heartfelt tributes. Jessica Jeffords was onstage next to the other friends of the fallen. She bit her lip nervously, sighed, and looked from side to side. It was clear that the stories of Powell and Bell were bringing up strong emotions.

But soon it was her turn, and she found the strength to speak.

"Sgt. Snyder was my best friend, the best friend I could ever ask for. She became my sister. She was a great leader and she was the same person in and outside of work. Snyder helped everyone. She was a hard worker and an even better leader. I always looked up to her. She was there for me through thick and the thin. She looked at things in life in a positive, upbeat way. She enjoyed seeing places, meeting new people, and definitely wasn't afraid to take on challenges. She enjoyed everything life had to offer...Friends like Snyder are very rare to find... Snyder was always up for new challenges. I remember one late night, we borrowed someone's manual car because she randomly wanted to learn to drive stick shift. I took her to this empty parking lot and tried teaching her. She couldn't multitask, focusing on the clutch and shifting at the same time. After stalling the car multiple times, and after a few months of practice, she eventually learned. She was definitely really clumsy, but always put a smile on my face. One day, after work, we went to the store to get some things. She was texting and walking at the same time and ran straight into a pole. She received a huge welt on her forehead from the pole. She always made me laugh. That's how I want everyone to remember her. She always put family first. I met her family for the first time a week ago and I felt like I already knew them because of all the wonderful things Snyder used to say about them. She was always on the phone with someone in her family every time we were together. I see a little bit of her in every one of her family. She impacted a countless number of people in a positive way. On her way back home, there were thousands of people lining the streets to pay their respects. She impacted people she never got the chance to meet. She'll be missed greatly but never forgotten."

After a song from a guitarist, the Chaplain said a few more words, quoting "dust in the wind." Then they all stood for a final roll call.

Standing with a clipboard, one of the sergeants began calling out names. Some soldiers who were present called out. Then he called the names of the fallen to show their absence. "Sgt. Snyder. *Pause.* Sgt. Devin Snyder. *Pause.* Sgt. Devin Arielle Snyder."

After three gunshots and the playing of taps, bagpipes played "Amazing Grace" as families and friends wept for their loss.

Jeffords spent a few days with Damien and Dineen who had been able to come. She insisted that their escort drive them around to Devin' favorite spots, including the place in the mountains where Devin used to find peace. Then they went home and the memorials were over.

Chapter 16: Blessings and Accidents

Summer lurched slowly along. Some of Devin's friends and track teammates painted a large rock on Interstate 390 with her portrait superimposed on an American flag. On the side, it read "RIP Devin Snyder." The rock, which had been painted over and over hundreds of times by local fraternities, was a sort of natural road sign sitting in full view of the highway.

Both Damien and Natasha were given a few weeks of leave. When the time was up, they had to return to their assignments.

"It was hard," said Natasha. "I didn't want to leave my mom but I also knew at the same time I needed to get back to my life. So I came down and I went back to work and tried to carry on my days as best as I possibly could, which was ridiculously hard."

The Navy considered Devin's death an insurmountable personal hardship and forbid Natasha from deploying any more. She had shore duty after that.

"I didn't even go on a ship," she said. "I was in a normal office every day."

One negative of shore duty was that she could drink. The lure of the bottle proved to be too attractive for Natasha, and she drowned her many sorrows. This went on for nearly a year. She was drinking everyday, sometimes at work. She was caught and reprimanded, but they understood that it was her grief that pushed her to seek the numbness of alcohol. She cut back but it wasn't clear that she had it totally under control.

"Within a month she found out she was pregnant," said Dineen. "I still say Kinsley was her lifesaver because then she knew she had something to live for."

Just over two years after Devin's death, Kinsley Arielle was born. Her blonde hair reminds everyone of Devin.

"She's an angel," said Ed. "I love that little girl. She's special."

Natasha has since had another daughter. Dineen swears the baby looks just like Devin in her baby pictures.

Damien struggled in his own way. He returned to rear detachment. Dealing with the daily frustrations of Army life became harder to do.

"He just became very angry," said Dineen. "He never used to be like that."

Fortunately, Damien ran into Sgt. Major Orvis. He knew the Snyders, since he was the one who helped Jessica Jeffords become the special escort. As the Sergeant Major on rear D, he offered advice and guidance for Damien as well.

"He told me to come over, so I went over and talked to him for a good bit of time," said Damien.

The talks helped Damien. Other soldiers who had known his sister reached out to him as well. It was good to know that he had support.

Later, he found more support in his wife, a fellow soldier. Now they have a son, named Devin.

Back home in Cohocton, the winds turned the wind turbines and brought flurries of snow along with Christmas lights and tinsel. Families gathered together, but as in the military funeral's final roll call, the family members who were missing were the most noticeable.

Just after Thanksgiving, Ed posted on Facebook a thank you to friends and family for their support and apologized for not getting personal thank you cards out sooner.

His Facebook posts from that time seemed to indicate that Devin was still very much in his daily thoughts. He explained his argument against the not very consoling idea that "everything happens for a reason." He wrote: "There is no reason to lose young people to war... no reason for cancer... and death should only be after living a full and fruitful life... so no I do not believe that things happen for a reason."

Later, he posted poems remembering her. He posted an obituary of another fallen soldier and decried the folly of the war. On Christmas, he posted a grief-stricken rant in all caps morning the loss of "a daughter who meant the world to me" as well as forty-seven of his friends in the Navy.

"Ed and Devin were so close and it just sent Ed in a tailspin when we lost her," remembered Dineen.

The Snyders got through Christmas and December 31ˢᵗ came. It was a warm day, so Dineen and Ed decided to drive the 4-wheelers up the hill and over the empty farm fields to Ed's cousin's house in Atlanta. People were drinking. People were laughing. It would only intensify later that night. Had people already forgotten her? Thoughts of bitterness, hopelessness, and carelessness entered Ed's mind.

They decided to ride home early, but since it was getting dark and cold quickly, they took the road home instead of the trails through the woods. They would end up past Dineen's parents' house on Davis Hollow Road, a winding back road that follows a tributary of the Cohocton River. Ed had been feeling that feeling again, the anger, the rage, the deep, screaming sadness that could only be quieted by the speed of the 4-wheeler. He took off, and the scream of the engine echoed the screaming inside. But it came back. He went even faster, opening up the throttle down the winding road, way ahead of Dineen, moving farther away from her.

"Oh, come on!" said Dineen, who was having difficulty keeping up.

Ed has a hard time communicating what he was thinking and feeling that night. Maybe he was just trying to get ahead of the feeling of dread. Maybe the speed lifted the weight of sadness from him. Maybe he thought he could leave it behind forever, that there was a cure.

But there was also a sharp bend in the road.

Without fear to restrain him, and propelled to take chances by a desire to escape his grief, Ed did not slow for the curve. He was speeding.

It is a common occurrence in rural areas for farmers to fertilize their fields on warm days in the winter. A field with the corn cut and the ground frozen is easily drivable, as long as there are not too many snow drifts. The fertilizer is a type of liquefied manure from one of the local dairies and it is spread by a kind of tanker truck that fan-sprays the manure from the back of the truck. The truck drives up and down the field until the tank is empty and then they repeat. Roads inevitably are coated with a light spray or splashing of the fertilizer as the trucks go in and out of the fields. The smell hangs powerfully in the air, but it must not have been noticeable to Ed, who also did not notice that some of the liquid fertilizer was on the road at the curve.

When Dineen caught up with him, his ATV was tipped over by the side of the road. She hurried to it, then quickly slowed.

Where'd he go? Did he get mad and he dump it, or what? she thought as she climbed off the ATV.

Then she saw his helmet along the bank but she couldn't see him in the dark because of his black jacket, black pants, and black boots.

"Ed!" she yelled, and ran to the other side of the bridge, looking over the railing.

She ran back, looking again where his helmet had fallen. A corner of a grey sweatshirt was the first thing she recognized as his.

"I realized I was looking at his body laying in the creek bed face down," recalled Dineen. "So I jumped over the guardrail, ran down, went in the creek myself, grabbed his head to get him out. It was very cold. I had his head on my lap and I could get him out but I didn't want to move because he would be submerged in the water."

She tried to make a call on her new phone, but was not yet used to it and the only number that she had programmed in was Ed's cousin, from whose house they had come.

"Hello?" she heard, and tried to talk in the phone.

But the sound of the person's voice was coming from the road. It was Mr. Decker, whose daughter had run track with Devin.

"Are you okay?" said Mr. Decker.

"No! Somebody please help me with him!" yelled Dineen.

Mr. Decker and his son hurriedly climbed down the embankment and helped pull Ed out of the creek. While he was on the bank, Dineen tried calling 9-1-1, but due to shock, ended up calling Ed's cousin again.

"Nick, I've got to get off the phone," she said. "I've got to call 9-1-1. There was an accident."

"No, Dineen stay on the phone with me," he said.

"No," said Dineen desperately.

"Where are you?" asked Nick.

"I'm on Davis Hollow Road."

Dineen heard sirens, but again in her shock she worried that the siren was for someone else, and that the Ambulance and Fire Company from another town would have to come. She hadn't even called 9-1-1 yet, so she hung up and started to call. The next thing she knew, Nick was standing there. He had already been driving to find them. He was a 9-1-1 dispatcher and had already called it over the radio. The local police heard the call, the ambulance, the fire fighters, and all of them responded in minutes.

Dineen saw Nick and was glad to see him, but was in shock and was still concerned about calling.

"Okay, I've got to call 9-1-1" she said.

"Dineen, I'm already here. They're coming," he said.

Ed had hit the guardrail, flipped over it and had come down directly on his helmet, on the top of his head. His helmet was not tightened all of the way and came off as he flipped back over, landing face down in the water. It was a cold and desolate baptism.

They say that if his helmet had stayed on, the mask might have filled with water and he might have drowned before Dineen could get there.

At first, the emergency responders didn't think anything was wrong with him. He had a cut on his knee, but was moving around. They rushed him to the hospital and found out he had a broken neck, broken back, and a brain bleed.

"When I got to the hospital they were yelling at him," remembered Dineen. "He was starting to get combative from the head trauma."

The vertebrae in his back had broken in such a way that the spinal cord was not damaged. Even still, surgery had its risks and the doctors gave him a five percent chance of walking again. His chances of living were only ten percent.

"I went up to the hospital the day after the accident," said Judge Snyder. "They had him in the ICU and he wouldn't listen to anybody. He wouldn't do anything."

Finally, Ed spoke up and told everyone to leave so he could talk to his uncle alone.

"Get me out of here," he said, after everyone had gone.

"Sorry Ed, I can't do it," said Judge Snyder. He knew that Ed, like many people, was terrified of hospitals and just wanted to get out and back to his normal life.

"You know, Ed, you're damn lucky. If you don't knock it off, you're not going to be lying in a hospital bed. You'll be lying six foot under, just like your father," said his uncle, the Judge. "I don't know why Dineen's here with you at this point because I would have left your ass a long time ago."

Ed had no choice but to listen to his uncle's harsh judgment. And since he knew his uncle was right, he had no choice but serve his sentence in recovery, though he didn't take to the restrictions very well. His memory was severely affected by the accident, but the first memory he has is of the nurse strapping him down to the bed so he would not get up to use the bathroom and walk on his injured foot. She wheeled him into the hallway and left him there for a minute to calm down.

The doctors performed tests on him routinely in order to check his recovery from the brain bleed and the back and neck surgery. His neck and head were in a halo style brace. He was in recovery for three months.

His heel is still broken. It hurts every day, but Ed refuses to take off work for another surgery to fix it. He's just happy to be walking at all.

"The doctors I guess still scratch their heads to this day as to how and why I'm still here and even walking," he said.

"Even in the emergency room, they had a team of doctors come down," said Dineen. "They said he had somebody watching out for him. He had an angel. There's just no way that this even could have happened any other way."

They both know who it was.

Part 4: Legacy

"There's a divinity that shapes our ends,
Rough-hew them how we will."
-Shakespeare, *Hamlet*

Chapter 17: The Global

As of the writing of this book, it is still unclear if the deaths of 2,392 American soldiers achieved the intended goals of Operation Enduring Freedom (OEF) in Afghanistan. In some ways, the goals were met. Osama bin Laden is dead and al Qaeda is no longer the powerful terrorist organization it once was. Sgt. Devin Snyder was only one of the thousands of soldiers who died for that cause. Thousands of families, thousands of neighborhoods and schools, thousands of towns or cities have experienced the same loss as Cohocton, and although they all want to believe that the war that took their loved one made a difference in the world, they don't all believe that. Neither do many of the veterans. It is hard to see the victory amidst so much loss.

According to the Defense Manpower Data Center (DMDC), one of the data wings of the Department of Defense, and their Defense Casualty Analysis System, the time the Devin was in Afghanistan was the most violent year of the war.[66] Of the total 2,392 US casualties in OEF, 1,544 were killed in four bloodiest years (2009-2012). In 2011, the year that Devin was killed, about 500 US soldiers died. About half were from the Army, like her. Thirty-one of those died in June, like she did.

Though about fifty women died in Operation Enduring Freedom, Devin was the only female soldier from Western New York. The only other female killed in Afghanistan from Upstate New York was Army Lt. Col. Jaimie E. Leonard, a 39-year old West Point graduate, who died June 8, 2013 when an Afghan soldier who she was training killed her.[67]

That story, of Lt. Col. Leonard, is another story that makes people pessimistic about the outcome of the war.

"I think it's pointless that we're over there," said Stacey Jordan. "We're training them to fight for themselves and fight the Taliban but half of them are turning around and blowing us up. We're dumping way too much money into it. I felt like our time over there was pointless."

Other veterans will privately say similar things. A poll[68] of over 1200 people conducted by The American Legion asked, "When our troops leave Afghanistan, what will have been our legacy there?"

Though one would expect the respondents of a poll on the American Legion website to view the war in favorable terms, 57% agreed to the statement: "We exacted revenge on Bin Laden, but did not significantly improve Afghanistan." 22% called the war "a mixed bag" with "numerous successes and failures." Only 2% called it a "success."

Civilians have a difficult time making their opinions known. Political correctness demands that they speak highly of the troops, but is hard to separate the war from the people fighting it. Their support for the troops, then, can sometimes be in direct conflict with support for the war itself.

"I am against war," said Meaghan Oas in an interview, reflecting on the war in Afghanistan. "I don't want our troops to be over there. They're dying left and right and you don't want to see that, but no matter what, they're over there doing that because that's what they chose to do. That's what they want to do and, no matter what, you support them. I'm definitely not for war by any means but you always support the troops."

Over 5,300 soldiers have been killed in the Global War on Terror to date. Each of those people, and the 1,500 non-hostile (accidental) deaths, and the over 52,000 wounded, wanted to serve our country just like Devin did. For a variety of reasons, they each chose to join the Armed Forces.

Wayland-Cohocton graduate and schoolmate David Saxton decided to become a cadet in the ROTC program at Niagara University and, after Devin's death, he became especially interested in Explosive Ordnance Disposal (EOD) because he realized that he could be part of the group who disables explosives that were set up to kill US soldiers.

"Once I heard she was killed by an IED," said David, "I remember asking 'Why?' Then I remember kind of realizing EOD's different because your job fundamentally is not to go kill people. EOD's primary job is to make sure that people make it back here."

When Saxton finally grieved for Devin, it was almost a year later. He was going for a drive to visit his grandfather's grave on Memorial Day and instead took a turn to Devin's. Finding it overwhelming, he drove the highway to the boulder painted with her portrait. He pulled over and wept.

"I probably just sat on the side of the road and just cried for forty-five straight minutes," he said. "Whimpering like a dog."

That release is what gave him a sense of purpose, however.

I am in the right place. There is no better place for me to be right now. This is where I should be, he thought.

"Then I went to camp right after that for where you really prove yourself in ROTC," he said. "When I was done with that I did way better than I ever anticipated and they were like 'oh my god Saxton's not a shitbag after all!'"

About a week after that, after processing those feelings of loss into pride and motivation, Saxton experienced the loss of another good friend in Afghanistan, this one from college.

"That one was so much different," he said. "I thought I understood it all and I thought that once I flushed everything out I was good. I could handle that if it happened again, god forbid, but damn. He just got married. I talked to him a couple weeks before that and he's gone."

For the tens of thousands of veterans, while the legacy of the war will in some ways be the memory of those who were killed, it will also be in the friendships that they've made. After the sand and stone that once filled hescos becomes just sand and stone again, after entire forward operating bases are packed up and shipped home, what endures are those bonds between soldiers.

"I think there is a million clichés for it and pretty much every single one of them is true," said Saxton. "Being able to rely on someone with your life to a hundred-ten percent all of the time. It's special. I think that's what brings you close together."

However, that can mean that life after the military takes a lot of adjustment. After being secure in that feeling for so long, and under such intense circumstances, it seems that veterans can feel like *no one* has their backs after they get out.

"You're used to so much," said Josh Pruitt. "You're used to the early days and the late nights. You're used to the camaraderie that you have with your battle buddies. It's kind of hard at first when you don't have that. It's a rough transition. You have your family, you have your friends, but there's a difference from your high school friends from the friends you make in the military. When you spend five years with people, especially when you spend a year with somebody on deployment in Afghanistan, you grow a bond that is unbreakable by any means whatsoever. So you miss that quite a bit."

"That's one thing I do miss," said Jeremy Johnson, who now works in a machine shop in Michigan. "I would go back to have it."

"I was thinking of joining the Guard cause I do miss it, I do," said Stacey Jordan.

In Sebastian Junger's book *War*, he chronicles the lives of soldiers in the Korengal Valley in Afghanistan, east of where Devin was killed. As an embedded reporter, Junger lived through short stints of the war and got to know the soldiers and their commitment to each other. He views the bond between soldiers not only as a sort of primal, social "feeling," one that is completely lost in modern industrial civilization, but also as survival instinct. He writes:

"The platoon *was* the faith, a greater cause that, if you focused on it entirely, made your fears go away. As a soldier, the thing you were most scared of was failing your brothers when they needed you, and compared to that, dying was easy... The defense of the tribe is an insanely compelling idea, and once you've been exposed to it, there's almost nothing else you'd rather do."[69]

Some soldiers, especially military police, seek to find that sense of camaraderie as firefighters or police officers.

"I think you can have that in civilian life, but it's along the lines of firefighters, police officers," said Jeremy Johnson. "They have that bond with other firefighters and police officers. They have your back."

Even when they do enter that kind of profession, adjustment to civilian life can be a challenge. Sgt. Enlow is now a deputy sheriff in Oklahoma, though he expresses mixed feelings about civilian life in his hometown.

"I'm trying desperately to get out of here as soon as possible," he said, half-jokingly. "I came back for family and I hate it, but it's okay."

Upon his return from Operation Anaconda, Andrew Exum described his return to civilian life as being "like an amputee feeling for his ghost leg." That feeling of being out of place or without some central part of oneself often leads to the isolation of the veteran. Exum himself observed that "soldiers largely live outside the mainstream culture and are outsiders."[70]

That kind of isolation is entirely unnecessary, of course. Far from being untrained workers when they get out, our veterans have many transferrable skills. A young man or woman who can lead a team or squad during a deployment to a hostile combat environment can certainly lead a group of employees in the business world where they are not being fired upon. A soldier who can disassemble a carbine can probably handle taking apart residential plumbing fixtures. It also seems fairly achievable for an officer to go from strategic analysis of enemy movements to strategic analysis of a rival company's brand and marketing techniques. We, as a nation, can do better to help these young men and women find success and meaning in their civilian lives.

On December 7th, 2016, outgoing President Barack Obama spoke at MacDill Air Force Base in Tampa Florida. He reflected on his administration's role in and the modest accomplishments of the GWOT:
"I believe that we must never hesitate to act when necessary, including unilaterally when necessary, against any imminent threats to our people. But I have also insisted that it is unwise and unsustainable to ask our military to build nations on the other side of the world, or resolve their internal conflicts, particularly in places where our forces become a magnet for terrorists and insurgencies... So today, there are less than 10,000 American troops in Afghanistan. Instead of being in the lead against the Taliban, Americans are now supporting 320,000 Afghan security forces who are defending their communities and supporting our counterterrorism efforts."

"Now, I don't want to paint too rosy a picture," he continued. "The situation in Afghanistan is still tough. War has been a part of life in Afghanistan for over 30 years, and the United States cannot eliminate the Taliban or end violence in that country. But what we can do is deny Al Qaeda a safe haven, and what we can do is support Afghans who want a better future, which is why we have worked not only with their military, but we've backed a unity government in Kabul. We've helped Afghan girls go to school. We've supported investments in health care and electricity and education. You have made a difference in Afghanistan, and America is safer for it."

But the Global War on Terror continues. Troops are still in both Afghanistan and Iraq, the Taliban has gained ground, ISIS has largely replaced al Qaeda, and with our massive military infrastructure in the Middle East, it is doubtful that we will ever permanently leave.

In terms of the future for the region and what it might hold, it is difficult to tell. Every four years, the National Intelligence Council creates a report called "Global Trends" which is "an unclassified strategic assessment of how key trends and uncertainties might shape the world over the next 20 years." Used to inform senior US leaders and the public, the Global Trends report this year does not offer much hope. At best it is a paradox:

"The achievements of the industrial and information ages are shaping a world to come that is both more dangerous and richer with opportunity than ever before. Whether promise or peril prevails will turn on the choices of humankind. The progress of the past decades is historic—connecting people, empowering individuals, groups, and states, and lifting a billion people out of poverty in the process. But this same progress also spawned shocks like the Arab Spring, the 2008 Global Financial Crisis, and the global rise of populist, anti-establishment politics. These shocks reveal how fragile the achievements have been, underscoring deep shifts in the global landscape that portend a dark and difficult near future."

In the section about the Middle East, the authors of the report predict "security competition" between Iran, Saudi Arabia, Turkey, and Israel, which might "involve" China, Russia, and the US. What this means is anyone's guess, and what will actually come to pass is uncertain, but this warning sounds a lot like a World War to anyone who looks closely enough at it. This continuation of war in the region will undoubtedly further exacerbate the refugee crisis, sending millions of civilians to foreign lands in search of safety. It will also contribute to continued income inequality, which will likely breed further resentment, providing the fertile ground for extremist groups to rise to power.[71]

Overall, it does not look good for the Middle East and because of our commitments and interests there, we will not be able to extract ourselves from the fray.

Devin had a chance to back down and she chose to go to war. Her medical condition would have allowed her to finish her time in the Army at home or away from the combat zone. She might have become an MP trainer in a warm location in the Southern United States where Raynaud's would never be a problem. She might have used the GI Bill to get a degree in law enforcement. She might have worn a State Troopers uniform. She might have been Sherriff. She might have been an investigator and wore a suit all day. She might have been a mother to fair-haired children with their mother's unparalleled resolve.

If any criticism can be leveled at her, it is that she might have been wiser. She might have seen the signs. She might have given in. But how wise can a 20-year-old be? And how could we judge her negatively for her persistence? However tragic, it was her most admirable trait.

Perhaps the most important thing to remember about all of this is the immense effect that the death of a single soldier can have on a community. And this happens every time a soldier dies. And this happens in those far off countries every time a civilian accidentally dies.

Our country is too full with grief. The world is too full with grief. Everywhere, lost loved ones are remembered and hidden wounds remain open. We lament the loss of so many young people. We can't help but wonder what these young people might have become, if they had had the chance.

Chapter 18: The Local

Cohocton and the rural areas of New York have largely followed the old saying, "The more things change, the more they stay the same." People continue to work, raise families on modest incomes, and find brief but precious moments of joy.

The local economy has changed little. Industries and opportunities remain scarce.

What sort of development is planned for Cohocton?

"Nothing right now," said former Mayor Tom Cox bluntly, with a slight tone of exasperation. "We've had several attempts at different things. It isn't the government putting a stop to it; it's the people."

There was a proposed gas station that was scrapped because one of the landowners wanted more money for his land, Cox reported. A Dollar General was kept from going in for the same reason. Cohocton was also considered for a new Bombardier factory, but could not (or would not) fund the infrastructure needed.

"People that have been here all their lives are afraid of change," said Cox.

It is no wonder that they do, since many of the changes in the area have been for the worse. Still, Cox has some hope.

"It would be nice to have some of the little shops that were back here, you know? What people don't see is basically anybody coming south is going to get off 390 in Cohocton to go to Naples, Canandaigua or anywhere into the Finger lakes. A lot of traffic goes through here so it'd be nice to get it back to a tourist area…but nobody seems interested in that."

It may just be a lack of capital, rather than a lack of interest. Cohocton is in Steuben County, part of the Southern Tier of New York, among some of the poorest counties in the state.

"We're working on a comprehensive plan right now and the comprehensive plan doesn't really give us a future," said Cox.

Home to a high percentage of Appalachian working class people, both occupationally and culturally, it is not uncommon to see pick-up trucks full of crews of tired men stop into gas stations for sodas, subs, and bags of chips. Others stop into Carey's at the end of the day for cases of beer. Yard sales adorn the lawns on nice weekends and country music blares from cars. Nearly every other lawn has a sign that declares the injustice of stricter gun laws and, oddly, a confederate flag might occasionally fly in the back of a passing dually, or adorn a shiny belt buckle. Trump signs and Gadsden flags abound.

One thing a working class kind of place resents is people living on welfare. It is a common refrain to blame the poor for Cohocton's condition.

"I don't condemn people that need help with food stamps or welfare," said Judge Snyder, "but we've got a lot of free-loaders, and that's what I see around here."

It is perhaps less the resentment of people on public assistance and more the lament for the decay of the work ethic that fueled the post-WWII boom that comes up in conversations with Cohoctonites.

"There is a split because you've got the ones that don't want to work that are still getting that income to go get their cigarettes and alcohol, and then you've got the ones that work their tails off and they're helping to keep these people alive and keep them going. There is a split," said Judge Snyder. "Two different people. It's sad but true."

"Of the village of Cohocton's 890 people, 71% are on poverty level," said former Mayor Cox. He then claimed that half of the people living at the poverty level were on welfare.

Current data suggests a slightly different story, though the overall picture is still not promising for those who wish to stay in Cohocton. Labor statistics are difficult to trust, but they are a reference point. People have a right to privacy about the programs in which they are enrolled, but some information is available.

Census data indicates that there are now over 1,000 residents of the village, comprised of 334 households. Median household income is $39,531, well above the federal poverty threshold for a family of four, which is about $24,000. Only 26.2% of Village of Cohocton residents are below poverty line.[72] The rest who may appear to be on some sort of public assistance, it seems, are simply among the ranks of the working poor.

According to data from a recent Freedom Of Information Law (FOIL) request to the Steuben County Department of Social Services, "case counts" for the Village of Cohocton are as follows: Temporary Assistance for Needy Families (TANF) 7, Supplemental Nutrition Assistance Program (SNAP) 79, and Medicaid 148. Each case could be one person or it could be a family. If we count each "case count" as a household, that would mean that 44% of households in the Village of Cohocton get public health care and about 24% get food stamps. Many of them are probably the same households. Only 2% get TANF, which is cash assistance for living expenses.

Fraud is said to be rampant, but it is impossible to verify. Some people might cheat to get the full 60 months of temporary assistance, while others might have a genuine disability. Some might try to exaggerate their disability. Others might be people who do work, but get government health care for their children. It is impossible to get a count because of the various social programs available to low income people in New York State. It is a wide net. Does that mean that anyone participating in any of those programs is "on welfare"? Maybe it does to some, but like anything else, there are shades, degrees to the definition. It is unclear if Cohocton has that many "freeloaders." Many seem to work enough to maintain their modest lifestyles. The high rates of enrollment in social programs are more likely tied to the steep economic decline of the rural areas in the last 30 years, not due to a moral decline in the individuals or families as some suggest.

Nevertheless, it is probably true that 25% of people in the Village of Cohocton get at least health care and food stamps. It is unclear how many receive housing benefits, but housing might be one of the few things that even a low-income family can afford in Cohocton.

"The high welfare rate comes from the low cost of housing," said former Mayor Cox. "If you're going to buy a house here it's low cost. You've got a lot of people that moved out and kept the property and they're renting it out or selling it off to-- I guess the term 'slumlord' works."

Not long ago, according to local reports, a construction firm came into the hamlets of North Cohocton and Atlanta and started buying up homes. They would fix the homes to basic standards, but then rent them out at low costs. Years would go by with little repair or maintenance, and the effect was that whole streets were left in disrepair.

"There are so many of them that used to be beautiful homes up through there that are worthless now. I wouldn't give ten thousand dollars for any one of them, and it's sad but that's what happened," said Judge Snyder.

As in other places, with poverty often comes heavy drug use. Rates of heroin and methamphetamine use has increased sharply in the rural areas of upstate New York, similar to what is happening in Vermont[73] and much of Appalachia.[74] The common belief is that there is a direct link between the over-prescription of opioids, leading to off-label abuse. This, in turn, leads to opioid addiction and makes heroin more attractive as a cheap alternative when the supply of opioid pills dries up.

"This kid next door just died two or three weeks ago," said Judge Snyder. "He could've gone on to bigger and better things. I hired him a couple times to come up to my house to do some lawn work. A hell of a worker."

What bigger and better things he might have done we'll never know, but we do know that his death is part of a larger trend in New York. According to a report done in June 2016 by the Office of the New York State Comptroller entitled *Prescription Opioid Abuse and Heroin Addiction in New York State*, "The 825 overdose deaths in which heroin was a contributing cause represented an increase of nearly 24 percent over the previous year, and almost 25 times the number recorded in the State ten years earlier."

If not an epidemic like other areas, heroin use is certainly a problem worth noticing. Local news outlets report drug arrests on the highway every week without fail. The same NYS Comptroller study above concludes that there was a "sharp jump in average annual use" from 2013-2014. During that time, "heroin use in New York … exceeded the national rate by nearly 50 percent."

Every once in a while, in one of the nearby counties, a driver is found passed out in a parking lot with a needle sticking out of his arm. The only way to save that person is for someone to give him a naloxone shot. In recent years, police officers, in addition to EMTs, have been trained to administer such life-saving shots. As of 2014, "2,036 officers have administered naloxone to over 3,100 individuals, saving the lives of nearly 90 percent of the individuals that required assistance."[75] In an attempt to make the overdose antidote more widely available, in 2017 New York Governor Andrew Cuomo set rules and allocated funds that made naloxone available for reduced cost or free to anyone without a prescription.

In 2015, SunEdison, who purchased First Wind for $2.4 billion, acquired the Cohocton wind farm.[76] SunEdison, perhaps due to the acquisition of too much debt, recently declared bankruptcy,[77] leaving the future of the wind farm uncertain, an all-too familiar status for industry and business in rural New York State.

In the depth of the valley, beneath the spinning blades of the wind farm, is the Mapleview Cemetery, which is home to many large maples with shaggy bark, that turn bright orange in the autumn sun. There are many flags on the graves, and many of the gravestones with flags have dates in the 1940s, around the time of WWII. The graveyard, like others, contains headstones of semi-permanent granite stone, monuments to the reality of human impermanence.

This cemetery is also home to the Veterans' Memorial, revealing another proud tradition of the area: military service. An artillery cannon sits out front. In the memorial itself is a giant American flag, surrounded by the flags of each branch of the military. Around the flags are brick walls and on the walls are mounted boards with the names of veterans from each of the wars in American history. For the Civil War, there is a Snyder. Under WWI, there is a Snyder. Under WWII, there are six Snyders. There are three Snyders listed under Vietnam. Ed Snyder, Devin's father, is listed in the peacetime section. For the Iraq and Afghanistan Wars, his children Natasha Snyder, Damien Snyder, and Devin Snyder are listed. Sadly, yet proudly, the fifth wall is empty, as if we expect there to be more names both to honor and to grieve in future wars.

The Snyder family carries on to this day with a greater appreciation for life. Devin's siblings have started families, Dineen advocates for better nutrition and exercise at school, and Ed works hard to maintain a positive outlook, but frequently buries himself in his work. Dineen, in many ways, is at the very center of this story. She has somehow found the personal strength to be supportive of her husband and children and yet remains positive, despite an apparent loss of faith.

"The Snyders still have a hard time coming to church," said Julie Martin.

Every November, for All Saints Day, the Zion Lutheran Church holds a memorial service in which people can send a memorial to anyone who has passed.

"The first year, Dineen came to church to send a prayer for Devin, but after that, it just became too hard," said Martin.

Perhaps due to the desire for something more concrete than the gospels can offer, Dineen and Ed visited a local medium. In a big, two-story home in a nearby town, Dineen and Ed see her in a room with creaky hardwood floors and several cats.

"She's good," said Dineen. "Devin comes out of her, like no kidding."

"We go every year," said Ed. "Once a year. We were big non-believers for the longest time, but not anymore."

In one visit, the medium told Ed and Dineen that Devin wanted them to get rid of a small picture of a little boy fishing in their bathroom. She also told them that their toilet was broke and running, and that Jessica, who had recently been visiting, was the one who broke it. It was as if Devin was teasing Jessica from the great beyond.

She spoke of Damien, too. She wondered why he was getting a motorcycle and said that he would hurt himself on it. The next year, he got a motorcycle. About a year after that, he crashed it.

"It's just bizarre," said Dineen, "but when we go it's kind of comforting."

"It's like we're talking to Devin through her," said Ed. "It's just the way Devin is, you can tell."

One of the most important questions that Dineen wanted to ask about Devin's death was whether or not Devin had been killed instantly, or if she had suffered greatly before she died.

"She said they went out that day and one minute she's riding in the back seat and the next minute grandpa is there," said Dineen. "She was just gone. That kind of confirmed it for me even though people had said it."

When they spoke about Ed's ATV accident, the medium told them that Devin was there. She had acted to save Ed because she did not want Dineen to go through two tragic losses in one year.

To Ed and Dineen, the bewilderment of the doctors only confirmed what the medium said.

"They cannot even fathom what happened," said Dineen.

The hospital staff had even suggested that Ed apply for social security disability because they did not think that he would ever work again. So, the Snyders filled out the paperwork and submitted it. Ed's recovery went remarkably well, and soon, they called the social security administration to cancel. Ed was out of the hospital in March. He had to wear a neck brace for a while, but there is a picture of him at about that time wearing the neck brace and sitting defiantly on his four-wheeler. He returned to work on April 18th.

The experience overall has changed him. Coming so close to death was part of it, but perhaps the more lasting effect was due to the belief that Devin had been there for him, that there is something after death.

"It makes you wake up," said Ed. "At the same time I'm not afraid to die but I don't want to die."

"I'm not either, now," said Dineen.

"You're here today and maybe not tomorrow," said Ed, "so you live today and if you wake up in the morning then you live that day, too."

Many people contributed to a variety of local memorials in order to honor her family's wish that Devin not be forgotten. Besides financial donations to the family, a number of stones, plaques, and paintings were created. One stone is near the library in Atlanta, another larger one is at the Lawrence Parks Recreation Area, where Devin used to work in the summer. A picnic pavilion there is also named in her honor. Farther north, on the side of the highway for all to see, a few of the girls who were friends with Devin in high school painted a large boulder with an American flag background and Devin's likeness in the center. Not long after that, despite the outrage of many people in the area and the owner of the land himself, a fraternity painted over the boulder with their letters, as part of a pledge week prank.

The stretch of the same highway that passes through Cohocton farther south was officially named "The Devin A. Snyder Memorial Highway." Former Town Supervisor Jack Zigenfus was part of the group who had that done.

"It took an act of the legislature," said Zigenfus. "We were pushing a deadline because the legislature was about to adjourn for the summer. You had to have the governor sign it. It was teamwork that made that happen."

A ceremony took place at the stone at Lawrence Parks Recreation Area and public officials unveiled the sign bearing her name. The next day, it was hanging up on the side of the highway, for all travelers to see. The highway runs east and west from there along the Cohocton River.

Some of those travelers might have been coming to the Fall Foliage Festival, where Coach Julie Martin and others renamed the soccer tournament the "Devin Snyder Memorial Spud Jug Classic."

Many of the girls who played soccer with Devin still come to town for the game. Mikayla Sick Rizzieri is pleased to get to see some of her old friends during that time.

"So I get to see them then and we get to talk about it and we get to cry together and hug and remember why we're there."

But the game is really about the current crop of girls. They pay tribute by wearing a specially made tournament jersey that is white and pink. All of the girls wear Devin's number one on the back. The girls, though they didn't know Devin, cheer for her at the beginning of the game. They use her legendary grit as motivation to play hard.

"Think about Devin!" Mikayla heard some of the girls say. "What do you think she would say guys? She wouldn't give up! We got to strive like those older girls would."

"It's great they all know how wonderful she is," said Mikayla, "but I wish they got to meet her. It brings me to tears every single time."

The Snyders award the Spud Jug to the winning team at the end of the game now, as well as MVP.

"The girls of course want to win that because it's the Devin Snyder most valuable player award and everybody knows she's a legend," said Mikayla.

"It's funny," said Judge Snyder. "I think her legacy is more in the high school. What she did in high school. The accomplishments there. The person that she was. I would find it hard to believe, even if people were a hundred percent totally honest, I don't think you could find one person that could say anything bad about her or didn't like her for some reason. Everybody was her friend."

Her legacy at the school is clear when scholarships are awarded in the spring, as there are two different memorial scholarships in her name. One was created from the money that was given to the family from the luminary and the other is funded by t-shirt and ticket sales from the Sergeant Devin A. Snyder Spud Jug Classic.

Her parents are also actively working to preserve Devin's memory through the Devin Snyder Memorial Foundation, which was established to help law enforcement and veterans. The focus of the foundation in the past few years has been project-based, but after recently establishing themselves as an official non-profit 501c3, the foundation is seeking to branch out to veterans' service organizations as well.

Funding for the foundation comes primarily from the annual "Ride to Remember." Motorcyclists from near and far converge on the small town of Wayland, NY to ride a memorial ride around the area where Devin grew up.

In 2014, at the second annual ride, over a hundred bikers gathered at the Wayland American Legion Post 402. Participants registered, were given a black t-shirt with a pink emblem on it, bought 50/50 tickets, and generally milled around the huge building and parking lot. It was a hot day. Sun shone off the chrome everywhere in the packed lot. Bikers hollered out to friends, people hugged and laughed, and flags hung quietly from back rests.

After a short wait, someone's voice finally came over the PA. A trio of local girls sang the national anthem. And then a special guest was introduced: Jessica Jeffords.

She said a few words, praised Devin, made a few jokes, and wished everyone a good ride. It was noticeably brief and ended abruptly.

"I started crying and then I had to walk away," she said later.

The ride began and went north, through the country roads that are familiar to those who hail from here. The hills are high and the valleys steep in the Finger Lakes region of New York State, and the route wound about them like a meandering snake. A long line of roaring engines flowed like a river of horsepower around the lakes and over the hills.

The ride continued south on various country roads to a route along Keuka Lake (a Native American name meaning "The Crooked Lake") to the village of Bath, where the Veterans' Affairs Medical Center is located. The facility looks like a small college campus, with giant oaks and a sprawling green lawn in a central square lined with walking paths and benches. It originated as the Grand Army of the Republic Soldiers and Sailors Home in 1878, but later was expanded to serve wounded combat veterans of New York State. Today, the Bath VA is a place of healing for veterans in the Southern Tier of New York and the Northern Tier of Pennsylvania. It is only appropriate that the ride pauses there each year.

The ride bears some resemblance to the motorcade for her homecoming. It is as if each June the motorcade returns, and for a short time, Devin rides home again. Veterans and friends come from all across the United States to be there.

Even the animals seem to know something important is happening. Red-tailed hawks, like feathered gargoyles, perch stoically on telephone poles to watch the motorcycles. As the parade of bikes entered the highway bearing her name, looking down from the height of the road into the little graveyard by the little white church the riders can see Devin's grave.

"When you're sitting on that motorcycle and there are 200 other motorcycles around you and you're being led by a cop, you

211

don't stop at any stoplights and you don't stop at any stop signs," said Meaghan Oas. "One year we went through Naples and saw veterans standing on the side of the street saluting us as we rode by. I cried. I cried the whole way through Naples. It's a good feeling. It's good and it's sad at the same time."

The ride has become so popular in the area due to the efforts of the volunteers. Donations are made yearly by local businesses for door prizes and raffles. The organizers of the event work hard to solicit donations and to provide an experience that appeals to bikers and non-bikers alike, veterans, and police.

"We have the best ride out there," said Greg McInnis, who serves on the foundation board. "What's kind of amazing is that there are no bikers in our club. What we've done is, we've been able to take non-biker people and put a great show on. We're always constantly changing and evolving...We need more help."

"A lot of the riders from the Patriot Guard come down every year," said Oas, "the same ones that escorted her home."

She recalled a moment a few years ago when she was coming out of a restaurant and she saw a man standing by her car looking at a sticker that said Devin's name and date of death. She walked up to him.

"Can I help you?"

"Did you know Devin?"

"Yeah, why?"

"I just wanted to let you know that I was on one of the motorcycles that helped bring her home."

"Thank you so much for doing that," she said, tearing up.

"I'm very sorry about your loss but I'm honored to have been a part of such a special day," the man told her.

While many might succumb to grief and let it consume them, the Snyders learned to turn their grief into opportunities for others.

Thanks to events like this, the Sgt. Devin Snyder Memorial Foundation is able to make donations and provide resources for local law enforcement. In February of 2014, the foundation was able to raise enough money to purchase a K9 for the Steuben County

Sherriff's office. The impressive German shepherd was imported from Holland and is named for Devin.

"Steuben only had one dog and he was on overtime all of the time," recalled Danette McInnis, who also serves on the foundation board. "They really needed one and they embraced it a hundred and ten percent."

The Devin Snyder Foundation has continued to support the Steuben County K9 program in the past few years with veterinary bills, police car modifications, and other expenses. The hope is to address the opioid epidemic, as well as the proliferation of methamphetamines, that poison rural life.

"It's ten-thousand dollars plus a commitment for the life of the dog and helping and the handler training and the canine Kevlar vest, and the kennel," said Greg. "It was a real cost."

The foundation, keeping in mind the things that Devin loved, is also looking into programs that provide therapy dogs to veterans with PTSD. In the future, the Devin Snyder Foundation will continue its work of healing and service through organizing fundraising events and donating those funds to important causes. They hope to maintain their momentum as they have by taking on new challenges.

Chapter 19: Memory and Absence

Ed, thinking of his retirement, dreams of a house near a beach where he can hear the sound of the water again. Perhaps one day, in the distant blue of the ocean, out where it meets the great blue sky, he'll see the color of Devin's eyes and feel her presence.

There are verifiable disembodied spirits who visit us in the world of flesh. Not ghosts, but the memory of those loved and lost. Their stories are part of who we are, part of our ongoing mythologies. They cannot be removed from us by their physical deaths, and thus as long as we live, so do they. They are what give us depth.

Devin's grave is less than a mile from the Snyders' home. Ed visits once a week or so. Above her grave is the highway that passes by their house. In the spring and summer rains, the traffic sounds vaguely like the rhythm of crashing surf, always present, like the feeling of loss.

Near the headstone is an American flag with a yellow ribbon tied to it that reads "Honor and Remember." The planters are full of blooming flowers in the summer, and bouquets have been placed around the stone. A figurine of an angel in prayer sits piously by, and an American Legion veteran marker reads "Afghanistan War Veteran." On the ledge of the stone, there are patches, a "Snyder" patch, a US Army patch, support our troops bracelets, and a pin. Engraved on the gravestone is the 164th MP company logo, two pistols behind a coat of arms. In the left corner are track shoes, and in the right corner is a soccer ball.

There rests the shieldmaiden of the Cohocton Valley.

These memorials help those who loved Devin Snyder to remember her. As the highway rolls past the small town with the small river at the center, her friends and family go on with their lives, knowing that the real memorials are not plaques or signs. They are the ones we build out of the substance of our own lives. Living a good life, it seems, might be the only way to truly honor the dead.

Acknowledgements

The idea to write this book came from Devin's mother, Dineen. I work with Dineen at Wayland-Cohocton Central School. She is now the Superintendent's Secretary, but at the time she was the computer lab monitor, and the printer was in that room, so I would walk down the hall several times a day to retrieve something I'd printed. She is a friendly woman and we would talk sometimes.

She would occasionally talk about her daughter. Sometimes it was about scholarships or upcoming events through the newly formed Devin Snyder Foundation. Each time she spoke, it was as if she was unburdening herself, bit by bit, of a deeply held, but secret sadness. It would come forth in breaks in her voice and deep sighs. She would look away and then look back with a smile that somehow only seemed to get stronger through the grief.

One day, somehow we got on the topic of Devin's story. Maybe it was about a newspaper article. She then dropped the hint.

"If only we could get someone we know to write a book," she said, raising her eyebrows and smiling.

"I'm someone you know," I said.

But I backtracked quickly and, unsure of what kind of commitment I might be making, told her that I would think about it and get back to her.

About a week later I was getting something at the printer again and she said that she and Ed had discussed and were wondering what I was thinking. I had been mulling it over the whole week. My heart was in it right away, but sometimes I can be easily excited about projects. I thought it would be a good thing to do for a gold star mother, and family, but I knew that if I did it, I would be going deep down the rabbit hole of a very sad story. As a teacher, I understood very well that sometimes knowledge can change a person, often for the better, but sometimes for the worse. So I wanted to be careful not to commit to something that I couldn't handle. I also didn't want to commit to something and then not complete it. Life is busy. I have a family and a career.

Eventually, I decided that it would have to be done over the course of several years, but that it could be done. And more importantly, I reasoned, it should be done. I told Dineen that I would start work on it that summer 2013, and by the fall, interviews began.

Dineen initiated most of those interviews. I am grateful for the discussions that I had with the Snyder Family, the McInnis Family, Jessica Jeffords, Stacey Jordan, Scott Enlow, Jeremiah Johnson, Josh Pruitt, Eric Hubbard, because they gave me a greater understanding of what members of our military and their families go through and what their lives are like. I must also thank Gregg Mark and Josh Farmer for helping me understand military language, culture, and procedures.

Many friends, teachers, and coaches of Devin's deserve thanks as well. Jeff Englert, Alyssa Englert, Emily (May) Duffy, Jen Harvey, Julie Martin, Kaya Rizzieri, Matt Bondgren, Meagan Oas, Mike Wetherbee, and Tyler Austin all generously gave their time. From them, I came to understand more clearly what the word community means.

I could not have put all of the information from those interviews together without Lanina Roby, who worked quickly and accurately on the transcriptions. Anne Markel's tough criticism and clear-minded guidance helped me shape the early draft, and I was able to resolve several problems with later drafts because of feedback from Mark Meyer, Alex Stearns, David Saxton, TJ Sparling, Kay Thomas, and others.

I'm thankful to the Wayland-Cohocton Central School District for years of support and for granting me a sabbatical to finish the manuscript. Livingston Arts was generous enough to provide financial support through an Individual Artist Grant, though my project may not have fit entirely with their funding priorities.

I would also like to thank my parents for their support and my dear wife for her unwavering understanding and encouragement.

Last, I must thank the troops for their service. For those who returned home, I wish that they understand that there is a reason for that. I hope they find their purposes in life and succeed. For those who did not return home, like the four others beside Devin who lost their lives on June 4, 2011, we will do our best to honor your sacrifice.

Endnotes

[1] Harak, G. Simon, S. J. "Why DID Iraq Invade Kuwait?"
http://mcadams.posc.mu.edu/blog/harak.html

[2] Johnson, Greg. "Kuwait Has Invested Oil Funds Prudently in U.S., Expert Says."
LA Times. http://articles.latimes.com/1990-08-21/business/fi-1057_1_kuwait-investment-office

[3] Gordon, Ilanit et al. "Oxytocin and the Development of Parenting in Humans." *Biological psychiatry* 68.4 (2010): 377–382. *PMC.* Web. 17 Mar. 2018.

[4] Bush, George and Brent Scowcroft. "Why We Didn't Go to Baghdad." *The Iraq War Reader,* 2003.

[5] "Subregions in Appalachia." *Appalachian Regional Commission.*
https://www.arc.gov/research/MapsofAppalachia.asp?MAP_ID=31

[6] "The Clinton-Sullivan Campaign of 1779." *National Park Service.*
https://www.nps.gov/fost/learn/historyculture/the-western-expedition-against-the-six-nations-1779.htm

[7] "The Clinton-Sullivan Campaign of 1779." *National Park Service.*
https://www.nps.gov/fost/learn/historyculture/the-western-expedition-against-the-six-nations-1779.htm

[8] *Old Trails on the Niagara Frontier* By Frank Hayward Severance

[9] *Classical Place Names in NYS* by William R. Farrell

[10] Moyers, Bill. *The Power of Myth.* Pg 116.

[11] Sauerbier Sprague, Kera. "A History of Cohocton." *Crooked Lake Review.*
http://www.crookedlakereview.com/articles/1_33/7oct1988/7sprague.html

[12] Greenspan, Jesse. "Remembering the 1993 World Trade Center Bombing."
History.com. http://www.history.com/news/remembering-the-1993-world-trade-center-bombing

[13] Gross, Christopher. "20 years later: Remembering the attack on Khobar Towers."
US Air Force.
http://www.af.mil/News/ArticleDisplay/tabid/223/Article/811370/20-years-later-remembering-the-attack-on-khobar-towers.aspx

[14] Rashid, Ahmed. "Global Jihad: The Arab-Aghans and Osama Bin Laden." *Taliban.*
Yale University Press, 2010.

[15] "1998 US Embassies in Africa Bombings Fast Facts." *CNN.*
http://www.cnn.com/2013/10/06/world/africa/africa-embassy-bombings-fast-facts/

[16] See Jean Piaget's theory of cognitive development

[17] See Erik Erikson's theory of psychosocial development

[18] Weaver, Mary Anne. "Lost at Tora Bora." *The New York Times.*
http://www.nytimes.com/2005/09/11/magazine/lost-at-tora-bora.html?_r=0

[19] *This Man's Army: A Soldier's Story from the Front Lines of the War on Terrorism,* Andrew Exum, 2004

[20] Exum, 132.

[21] "Wetmiller Dairy" *The Cohocton Journal.* Issue 1, Vol 42. February 2014.

[22] Roach, John. "Foliage, Tree Sitters Star in Appalachian Festival." *National Geographic News,* 6 October 2005.

http://news.nationalgeographic.com/news/2005/10/1006_051006_tree_sitters.html

[23] "Saddam addresses Iraqi people." *CNN*, 20 March 2003.
http://www.cnn.com/2003/WORLD/meast/03/20/irq.war.saddam.transcript/

[24] "Rumsfeld Declares Major Combat Over in Afghanistan." *Fox News*. 1 May 2003.
http://www.foxnews.com/story/2003/05/01/rumsfeld-declares-major-combat-over-in-afghanistan.html

[25] "Bush Says Major Combat in Iraq Over." *Fox News*. 2 May 2003.
http://www.foxnews.com/story/2003/05/02/bush-says-major-combat-in-iraq-over.html

[26] Otterman, Sharon. "Afghanistan: The New Constitution." *Council on Foreign Relations*. 3 February 2005. http://www.cfr.org/afghanistan/afghanistan-new-constitution/p7710#p0

[27] Whitaker, Brian. "Taliban murders voters to derail election." *The Guardian*. 27 June 2004. https://www.theguardian.com/world/2004/jun/28/afghanistan.brianwhitaker

[28] Katzman, Kenneth. "Afghanistan: Presidential and Parliamentary Elections." *Congressional Research Service Report*. 8 April 2005.

[29] "Cohocton Wind Farm." *The Wind Power*. 13 December 2017.
http://www.thewindpower.net/windfarm_en_4397_cohocton-wind-farm.php

[30] "July 7 2005 London Bombings Fast Facts." *CNN*. 29 June 2017.
http://www.cnn.com/2013/11/06/world/europe/july-7-2005-london-bombings-fast-facts/

[31] "Joint Declaration of the United States-Afghanistan Strategic Partnership." *Office of the Press Secretary*. 23 May 2005.
https://2001-2009.state.gov/p/sca/rls/pr/2005/46628.htm

[32] MacAskill, Ewen and Michael Howard. "How Saddam died on the gallows." *The Guardian*. 31 December 2006.
https://www.theguardian.com/world/2007/jan/01/iraq.iraqtimeline

[33] "Basic Military Police Course." *United States Army Military Police School*.
http://www.wood.army.mil/usamps/Training/BMPC31B.html

[34] MacAskill, Ewen. "Obama promises 10,000 more troops for Afghanistan." *The Guardian*. 14 July 2008.
https://www.theguardian.com/world/2008/jul/15/barackobama.usa1

[35] "Alaska's Mount Redoubt Erupts Six Times." *Fox News*. 24 March 2009.
http://www.foxnews.com/story/2009/03/24/alaska-mount-redoubt-erupts-six-times.html

[36] "Transcript: Obama Announces New Afghanistan, Pakistan Strategies." *Washington Post*. 27 March 2009. http://www.washingtonpost.com/wp-dyn/content/article/2009/03/27/AR2009032700891.html

[37] "Stanley A. McChrystal." *Biography*. http://www.biography.com/people/stanley-mcchrystal-578710#synopsis

[38] "Foreign Assistance in Afghanistan." *Foreignassistance.gov*. US State Department.
http://beta.foreignassistance.gov/explore/country/Afghanistan

[39] "Transcript of Obama speech on Afghanistan." *CNN*. 2 December 2009.
http://www.cnn.com/2009/POLITICS/12/01/obama.afghanistan.speech.transcript/index.html

[40] Simpich, Frederick. "Everyday Life in Afghanistan." *National Geographic*, Jan. 1921,

pgs 85-110.

[41] "Alexander the Great." *Cultural Property Training Resource: Afghanistan.* Colorado State University. https://www.cemml.colostate.edu/cultural/09476/afgh02-04enl.html

[42] "Alexander the Great." *Cultural Property Training Resource: Afghanistan.* Colorado State University. https://www.cemml.colostate.edu/cultural/09476/afgh02-10enl.html

[43] Simpson, John. "In Search of Afghanistan's Lapis Lazuli." *The Telegraph.* 2015. http://www.telegraph.co.uk/luxury/travel/63922/john-simpson-in-search-of-afghanistans-lapis-lazuli.html

[44] Risen, James. "U.S. Identifies Vast Mineral Riches in Afghanistan." *The New York Times.* 13 June 2010. http://www.nytimes.com/2010/06/14/world/asia/14minerals.html

[45] "Tesla Gigafactory." *Tesla.* 2018. https://www.tesla.com/gigafactory

[46] Dowd, Alan. "Afghanistan's Rare Earth Element Bonanza." *American Enterprise Institute.* 13 August 2013. https://www.aei.org/publication/afghanistans-rare-earth-element-bonanza/

[47] "Taliban offer 'security' for copper, gas projects." *Al Jazeera.* 29 November 2016. http://www.aljazeera.com/news/2016/11/taliban-offers-security-copper-gas-projects-161129131200604.html

[48] Woodward, Bob. *Bush at War.*

[49] Sarhaddi Nelson, Soraya. "Taliban Wages War on Afghan Girls' Schools." *NPR.* 5 April 2007. http://www.npr.org/templates/story/story.php?storyId=9396748

[50] "Pashtunwali." *Afghanistan Language and Culture Program.* San Diego State University. https://larc.sdsu.edu/alcp/resources/afghanistan/culture-2/pashtunwali/
The website further states that "Those who fail to fulfill the obligations of Pakhtu (self-respect) by wiping out insult with insult, lose their prestige in the eyes of their compatriots, render themselves liable to Paighore (reproach) and earn an unfair name." Therefore, the punishment of the boy may have been more for the vindication of the wronged party than to teach the boy a lesson.

[51] Goldman, Russell. "Who Is Terry Jones? Pastor Behind 'Burn a Koran Day'." *ABC News.* 7 September 2010. http://abcnews.go.com/US/terry-jones-pastor-burn-koran-day/story?id=11575665

[52] Peter, Tom A. "Why did Karzai spotlight Terry Jones's Quran burning?" *The Christian Science Monitor.* 5 April 2011. http://www.csmonitor.com/World/Asia-South-Central/2011/0405/Why-did-Karzai-spotlight-Terry-Jones-s-Quran-burning

[53] Singer, Peter W. "The Evolution of Improvised Explosive Devices (IEDs)." *The Brookings Institution.* 7 February 2012. https://www.brookings.edu/articles/the-evolution-of-improvised-explosive-devices-ieds/

[54] Lamothe. Dan. "The legacy of JIEDDO, the disappearing Pentagon organization that fought roadside bombs." *The Washington Post.* 17 March 2015. https://www.washingtonpost.com/news/checkpoint/wp/2015/03/17/the-legacy-of-jieddo-the-disappearing-pentagon-organization-that-fought-roadside-bombs/?utm_term=.f1e73d1658af

[55] "SEAL's first-hand account of bin Laden killing." *CBS News.* 24 September 2012. http://www.cbsnews.com/news/seals-first-hand-account-of-bin-laden-killing/

[56] Baker, Peter, Helene Cooper and Mark Mazetti. "Bin Laden is Dead, Obama Says." *The New York Times.* 1 May 2011.

http://www.nytimes.com/2011/05/02/world/asia/osama-bin-laden-is-killed.html

[57] "Oshkosh MRAP All Terrain Vehicle." *Army Technology*. 2018. http://www.army-technology.com/projects/oshkosh-mrap/

[58] "Oshkosh Defense To Deliver Additional M-ATV Protection Kits." *Oshkosh Defense*. 11 February 2011. https://oshkoshdefense.com/news/oshkosh-defense-to-deliver-additional-m-atv-protection-kits/

[59] Robson, Seth. "Army soon to field double-V hull Strykers to protect against blasts." *Stars and Stripes*. 20 May 2011. https://www.stripes.com/news/army-soon-to-field-double-v-hull-strykers-to-protect-against-blasts-1.144074

[60] Most of this is a composite of the sworn statements of about eighteen service members from reports obtained by the Snyders. It is important to remember that much of this happened in a very short span of time. I have slowed it down some for this narrative. Also, some of the information was redacted from the reports, so any gaps in the story are reflective of the gaps in the public record. All quotes are taken from the written record or from first-hand testimony.

[61] "Pre-Combat Inspection (PCI)." *Fort Hood*. US Army. http://www.hood.army.mil/leaders/csm/pci-pcc.pdf

[62] "DynCorp International Awarded Afghan Training and Mentoring Contracts." *DynCorp International*. 8 January 2015. http://www.dyn-intl.com/news-events/press-release/dyncorp-international-awarded-afghan-training-and-mentoring-contracts/

[63] Morris, Peter. "President's week ahead tips to global issues." *The 1600 Report*. CNN. 5 June 2011. http://whitehouse.blogs.cnn.com/2011/06/05/

[64] "Readout of the President's Monthly Meeting on Afghanistan and Pakistan." *Office of the Press Secretary*. The White House. 6 June 2011. https://obamawhitehouse.archives.gov/the-press-office/2011/06/06/readout-presidents-monthly-meeting-afghanistan-and-pakistan

[65] http://www.godhatesfags.com

[66] *Defense Casualty Analysis System*. https://www.dmdc.osd.mil/dcas/pages/casualties.xhtml

[67] "Army Lt. Col. Jaimie E. Leonard." *Military Times*. http://thefallen.militarytimes.com/army-lt-col-jaimie-e-leonard/6568467

[68] "When our troops leave Afghanistan, what will have been our legacy there? (Poll)." *American Legion*. 2018. https://www.legion.org/landingzone/217793/when-our-troops-leave-afghanistan-what-will-have-been-our-legacy-there

[69] Junger, Sebastian. *War*. 210-214.

[70] Exum, 206-207

[71] "Middle East and North Africa." *Global Trends Report*. Office of the Director of National Intelligence. 2018. https://www.dni.gov/index.php/the-next-five-years/middle-east-and-north-africa

[72] "Cohocton, NY." *Census Reporter*. 2015. https://censusreporter.org/profiles/16000US3616727-cohocton-ny/

[73] Seelye, Katherine. "In Annual Speech, Vermont Governor Shifts Focus to Drug Abuse." *The New York Times*. 8 January 2014. https://www.nytimes.com/2014/01/09/us/in-annual-speech-vermont-governor-shifts-focus-to-drug-abuse.html?_r=0

[74] Khazan, Olga. "The New Heroin Epidemic." *The Atlantic*. 30 October 2014.

https://www.theatlantic.com/health/archive/2014/10/the-new-heroin-epidemic/382020/

[75] "Governor Cuomo Announces No-Cost or Lower-Cost Naloxone Available at Pharmacies Across New York." *Governor's Press Office*. 7 August 2017. https://www.governor.ny.gov/news/governor-cuomo-announces-no-cost-or-lower-cost-naloxone-available-pharmacies-across-new-york

[76] "SunEdison finalizes $2.4bn acquisition of First Wind." *ReCharge*. 29 January 2015. http://www.rechargenews.com/wind/870448/sunedison-finalises-usd-24bn-acquisition-of-first-wind

[77] "Maine wind power developer SunEdison files for bankruptcy protection." *Portland Press Herald*. 21 April 2016. http://www.pressherald.com/2016/04/21/one-time-star-in-solar-energy-sunedison-files-for-bankruptcy-protection/